YOUR PASSPORT TO
INTERNATIONAL
LIBRARIANSHIP

ALA Editions purchases fund advocacy, awareness,
and accreditation programs for library professionals worldwide.

YOUR PASSPORT TO
INTERNATIONAL
LIBRARIANSHIP

CATE CARLYLE
DEE WINN

ALA Editions
CHICAGO | 2018

CATE CARLYLE is the Curriculum Resource Centre coordinator at Mount Saint Vincent University in Halifax, Nova Scotia. She is currently a special academic librarian and children's book reviewer, and she formerly served as an elementary schoolteacher, school librarian, and public library assistant. She volunteers regularly for various causes, has volunteered in libraries in Canada, Guatemala, Honduras, and Nicaragua, and has written articles and conference presentations on international volunteerism.

DEE WINN is the head of information services at Concordia University Library in Montreal, Quebec. She has worked as an academic librarian in Vancouver, British Columbia and Windsor, Ontario. She has visited libraries on five continents and volunteered in a school library in Guatemala. Before becoming an academic librarian, she was an elementary schoolteacher in Atlanta, Georgia.

© 2018 by the American Library Association

Extensive effort has gone into ensuring the reliability of the information in this book; however, the publisher makes no warranty, express or implied, with respect to the material contained herein.

ISBN: 978-0-8389-1718-3 (paper)

Library of Congress Cataloging-in-Publication Data
Names: Carlyle, Cate, author. | Winn, Dee, author.
Title: Your passport to international librarianship / Cate Carlyle, Dee Winn.
Description: Chicago : ALA Editions, an imprint of the American Library
   Association, 2018. | Includes bibliographical references.
Identifiers: LCCN 2018006317 | ISBN 9780838917183 (paperback : alk. paper)
Subjects: LCSH: International librarianship—Vocational guidance. | Volunteer
   workers in libraries—Foreign countries. | Voluntarism—International
   cooperation.
Classification: LCC Z672.3 .C37 2018 | DDC 020.6/21023—dc23 LC record available at
https://lccn.loc.gov/2018006317

Book design by Kimberly Thornton in the Alda, Freight Sans, and King typefaces. Cover images © Adobe Stock.

♾ This paper meets the requirements of ANSI/NISO Z39.48–1992 (Permanence of Paper).

Printed in the United States of America

22 21 20 19 18   5 4 3 2 1

The world is a book
and those who do not travel
read only one page.

—*Saint Augustine*

contents

acknowledgments

Thank you to Librarians Without Borders' Guatemala program manager,· Debbie Chavez, for contributing chapter 7 of this book.

Thank you to the following LIS professionals who graciously contributed their reflections and advice:

Celia Avila

Dianne Cmor

Sarah Gibson

Mairead Mooney

Dora A. Domínguez Piedrasanta

Jorge Rivera

Philip Segall

Sarah Stang

Christina Wilson

introduction

Today Is the Day

DESPITE THE BEST EFFORTS OF LIBRARY AND INFORMATION SCIENCE (LIS) professionals, the classic librarian stereotype still exists; that of the older obsessive female, hair in a bun, glasses on a chain around her neck, shushing visitors. This stereotype can be seen in movies, television shows, books, and online, but it is not an accurate depiction of library and information professionals in this century. Today's professionals cannot be placed into neat boxes; we represent all walks of life and are found in all corners of the globe. We are a diverse group of engaged, passionate, educated men and women who speak many languages and hold differing beliefs. Our interests range from classical music to grunge rock, graphic novels to zines, impressionist art to graffiti, coding to web design, fast food to haute cuisine, conservative to liberal and Green, and Christian to Wiccan. You may very well find some of us behind the counter wearing glasses, but we can just as likely be found roaming our maker spaces, tablet at the ready, proudly sporting unicorn hair, tattoos, and piercings.

Just as the typical librarian has changed, so too has the librarian's role. We are no longer solely book checkers and noise monitors; we are committed to improving our communities and our world. We thrive on empowering our users and making a difference. We are committed to open information, literacy, knowledge, health, social justice, prosperity, civil rights, and the eradication of poverty. Our interests are not confined to our libraries' four walls and shelves of books. We are global thinkers and doers, movers and shakers. If you have picked up this book, then you may be (1) an LIS professional who is interested in broadening your horizons and making a change for the better in our troubled world, (2) someone from another profession who is committed to volunteering, or (3) someone looking for an interesting read, or (quite possibly) our proud friends, family, and colleagues. We wrote this book not only because we wish such a book had existed when we were scrambling to plan our first international volunteer trips, but also because we felt there was a need for this resource. Our goal is to provide you with the practical information, helpful tips, and insights from experienced international volunteers that you will need to ensure a successful trip. We hope that our stories and advice inspire you, and we hope you will share your time and talents with those in need, open your eyes and heart to new experiences, see all that this world has to offer, and leave it a better place. You can do it. Get started. Get out there. You won't regret it. As the old saying goes, "A year from now you will be glad you started today."

Bon voyage!
Cate and Dee

chapter 1

Everything You Need to Know about International Librarianship (and More)

What Is International Librarianship?

When you hear someone refer to "international librarianship," what do you think of? A librarian who is originally from one country but is working in a different one? An organization that donates books to libraries in developing countries? A course that you took years ago, while earning your MLIS degree, but haven't thought about since? The international organization Bibliothèques Sans Frontières? Different people use the phrase "international librarianship" to mean many different things, so we thought we would begin by explaining exactly what we mean when we use the term. Numerous librarians and scholars have noticed (and criticized) the American English tendency to define the word "international" as meaning "someone or something from another country." As a result, anything that is not American is international. This differs from how the word is defined in British English, which uses the term "foreign."[1] When you think of the word "international," which definition comes to mind? J. Stephen Parker published the most widely accepted definition of international librarianship (IL) in 1974, and we have decided to use it here too:

> International librarianship consists of activities carried out among or between governmental or non-governmental institutions, organiza-

tions, groups, or individuals of two or more nations, to promote, establish, develop, maintain, and evaluate library, documentation and allied services, and librarianship and the library profession generally, in any part of the world.[2]

Although Parker doesn't use the word "partnership," we believe that the most important element of IL is that it is a partnership between individuals or organizations from different countries who work together to achieve a shared goal. It is the emphasis on collaboration that distinguishes IL from charity work, because true IL goes beyond libraries or librarians from a developed country simply raising funds or donating books to a library in a developing country; it implies establishing a long-term, mutually beneficial partnership. People with an interest in international librarianship are usually curious or concerned about equitable access to information and the development of libraries and related services around the world.

A Rose by Any Other Name

Because you frequently see the terms used simultaneously, if not interchangeably, no discussion of international librarianship is complete without also considering "comparative librarianship" (CL). Danton's (1974) definition of CL is still regarded as the most authoritative one to date and asserts that comparative librarianship is an

> area of scholarly investigation and research [that] may be defined as the analysis of libraries, library systems, some aspect of librarianship, or library problems in two or more national, cultural, or societal environments, in terms of socio-political, economic, cultural, ideological, and historical contexts. This analysis is for the purpose of understanding the underlying similarities and differences and for determining explanations of the differences, with the ultimate aim of trying to arrive at valid generalizations and principles.[3]

When we unpack this definition and compare it to the definition of IL, we clearly see that the main differences are that CL is inherently considered academic, and it aims to identify and analyze the major similarities and differences between two or more distinct environments, while IL is comprised of collaborative work between partners in two or more countries. In the 1980s, the term "world librarianship" was used as an alternative for "international librarianship," and in the twenty-first century the use of the phrase "global librarianship" has increased significantly in library literature.[4] We recognize the history and importance of these other terms, but we believe that the term "international librarianship" best reflects our experiences.

Before participating in an international volunteer project, it is important to consider the economic, cultural, and political context facing the foreign library in which you will be working. As a volunteer, you don't want to advocate for procedures, policies, and practices that are effective at the library where you are employed, but which would prove unsustainable or otherwise ineffective in the library where you are volunteering. The most reputable international volunteer projects feature collaboration with local community

The Evolving Nature of International Librarianship

FOR ME, AS a child, the term "international" was exotic, foreign, and a bit scary. It embodied scratchy phone calls to overseas relatives, fragile blue airmail letters, and summer nights spent watching airplane arrivals with my father on the roof of Toronto's Pearson Airport as we awaited our relatives from the United Kingdom. If I could Freaky Friday back to my younger self, she would not believe the places I have traveled and the things I have seen. The term "international" has changed significantly for me with the advent of online communication, quick and inexpensive travel, and people constantly on the go. Cultures have migrated and integrated, and information is shared globally in the blink of an eye. The term "librarianship" has also changed greatly in my lifetime: it has morphed from my reading Pat Hutchins's Titch under the circulation desk while my mother checked out books in our local library in the 1970s, to today's book-vending machines, drag queen story times, and virtual librarians. With these changes in the LIS profession and given what we now consider "international," there is no question in my mind that "international librarianship" as a whole will continue to evolve as well. The sky is the limit.

Cate Carlyle, Nova Scotia, Canada

members to ensure that the projects meet their needs and seek to implement sustainable solutions.

Approaches to International Librarianship

We have presented a working definition of international librarianship, but we recognize that there are degrees of IL, and scholars and practitioners have been working to identify and refine these distinctions since the 1970s. In her recent article, Sellar argued that there are four different approaches to IL: international-immersion, charitable projects, other study, and reciprocal, cooperative relationships.[5] International-immersion refers to activities that librarians may undertake on their own, such as subscribing to discussion lists that include librarians from a variety of countries, preparing multilingual subject guides for international students, attending an international conference, or going to a conference in a country in which they do not work or live. Many types of international projects are charitable in nature. You will recognize them as projects where a library, a librarian, or an organization from a developed country donates goods (usually books) or funds to a counterpart in a developing country. Although this type of work may be beneficial to the library that is on the receiving end, it is not a reciprocal relationship. The "other study" approach involves work that describes libraries (their conditions, practices, staff, successes and challenges, etc.) in foreign countries. This includes journal articles with titles such as "The Future of Public Libraries in Botswana" or "An Analysis of Reference Services among Academic Libraries in Brazil." Reciprocal, cooperative relationships feature collaborators from different countries working on a shared goal. Ideally, a partnership is created and sustained over a period of time. Some examples of this approach are shared in Chapter 3.

INTERNATIONAL LIBRARIANSHIP ACTIVITIES

There are a wide variety of IL activities that librarians can participate in, and the good news is that many of these activities don't require a passport. One of the easiest ways to satisfy your interest in IL is to subscribe to an IL discussion list. You read that right: discussion list. Discussion lists are still a useful communication tool for receiving relevant news, updates, and messages in your particular areas of interest. For example, the International Federation of Library Associations and Institutions (IFLA)'s discussion list is described as "an electronic forum intended to foster communications between IFLA, its membership, and members of the international library community. The goal in establishing this list is to facilitate information exchange as well as professional communication and development within the IFLA community."[6] (For a list of other IL discussion lists, see chapter 8.) A recent look through the IFLA archive shows that information on the following was shared: a new report entitled "Development and Access to Information," an update on IFLA's Global Vision Discussion, conference registration reminders, an invitation to tour a prison library in Poland (at the annual IFLA conference), and various announcements about new open-access publications, courses, competitions, and giveaways.

Another way to engage with the IL community from the comfort of your own couch is to read IL research. You never know: even just taking the time to read a few articles could inspire you to set out on a new adventure or lead to a new research interest. If reading about IL whets your appetite and you find yourself wanting more, you could consider writing an article and submitting it to any of the journals noted above for publication. If publishing in a peer-reviewed journal is daunting, you could also consider publishing in an LIS magazine, an LIS zine, in your state or provincial library association's newsletter, or in an online forum or blog.

International Librarianship Journals

THERE ARE MANY specialized journals to choose from, including:

- *Focus on International Library and Information Work*
- *International Federation of Library Associations (IFLA) Journal*
- *International Journal of Librarianship*
- *International Journal of Librarianship and Administration*
- *International Journal of Library and Information Science*
- *International Library Review*
- *International Research: Journal of Library and Information Science*
- *Perspectives in International Librarianship*

On the other hand, if your passport is valid and you have extra time and money available, you could consider attending a conference abroad. This is one of the best ways to learn firsthand about the opportunities and challenges facing libraries (and librarians) in other countries. You will also become aware of innovative programs and initiatives that have proven successful, and you will be exposed to exceptional networking opportunities as you meet librarians from around the world. Additional ways to use your passport to immerse yourself in the IL world are to work abroad, participate in a library exchange, take a study trip or sabbatical to another country, or join (and become active in) an international professional organization.

International Librarianship in Action

When thinking about volunteering in an international library, you may find yourself wondering, "Why is there a need for volunteers in libraries around

Librarians as a Global Force

I AM AN enthusiastic advocate for international librarianship. I have been very fortunate to be able to participate in projects such as Cycling for Libraries, LIS International Summer School in Stuttgart, and the International Librarians Network. My experiences as a volunteer have, above all, shown me how united we are in the values and ideas we share as library and information professionals.

Librarianship faces an uncertain future. My hope is that librarians can increasingly work as a global force to protect free, unbiased information in this era of "fake news," threats to net neutrality, and increasing censorship worldwide. The right to "seek, receive, and impart information and ideas" is, after all, a basic human freedom as set out in the UN's Universal Declaration of Human Rights (Article 19).

At a time when abundant misinformation is being disseminated ever faster and more widely across the Internet, collaborating in any ways we can across national borders becomes even more important to protecting both our combined knowledge and our shared fundamental rights.

Philip Segall, England, UK

the world?" As Sharma has explained, although most libraries in developed countries have leveraged the use of technology to provide outstanding services and resources to their patrons, this is not the case in developing countries. "Many countries in Africa, Asia, the Middle East, and South America are trying to introduce technology in their libraries, but a majority of them are still behind because of lack of funds and initiative from their rulers and political leaders, poverty, hunger, illiteracy, war, famines, and poor planning."[7] The need for international volunteers in libraries has arisen as a direct result of these challenging conditions, and when programs are implemented effectively, they are an important way to alleviate the negative consequences of these extremely difficult and complex circumstances.

Two organizations running successful programs that include an international librarianship component are the Canadian Organization for Development through Education (CODE) and Libraries Without Borders. CODE was established in 1959, and has grown to become Canada's preeminent international development agency dedicated exclusively to improving educational opportunities for children around the world. It accomplishes its goals by establishing strategic partnerships with local schools and by implementing a number of other initiatives, such as collaborating with teachers, librarians, and publishers to support local children's book production; assisting with teacher training; and establishing book awards. Although CODE does not have opportunities available for librarians who want to volunteer, anyone is able to collaborate with them through their Adopt a Library project. Adopting a library involves fund-raising to purchase books, shelves, furniture, and training for library staff.

Libraries Without Borders' mission is to "work to ensure that regardless of their circumstances, people throughout the world can live with dignity and the opportunity to thrive through access to information, education, and culture."[8] They work to achieve this goal by providing access to information following emergencies and in post-conflict areas; advocating for the establishment of libraries and access to free educational resources; and using libraries to inspire entrepreneurship and social change. Libraries Without Borders is currently working in countries as diverse as Australia, Iraq, Rwanda, Colombia, France, and the United States.

LIBRARIANS' THOUGHTS ON INTERNATIONAL LIBRARIANSHIP

In 2016, Karen Bordonaro conducted comprehensive research to investigate librarians' thoughts, feelings, attitudes, and experiences with international librarianship. She surveyed 320 librarians from across the globe and held individual interviews with 25 of them.[9] Her research indicates that librarians have extremely positive feelings toward IL. In response to the survey

On International Librarianship

FOR ME, INTERNATIONAL librarianship represents the intersection of three of my favorite activities—librarianship, volunteering, and traveling; and as a result, it is a natural fit for me. That doesn't mean that I immediately recognized these connections when I began my library career; in fact, I didn't. What it does mean is that I've been lucky enough to be able to integrate my lifelong passions with my professional work. Volunteer work has always been an important and meaningful part of my life. My secondary school had a Rotaract Club that participated in numerous local volunteer projects and held fund-raisers for international programs every year. My experiences with that club sowed the seeds that led me to become passionate about and dedicated to volunteer work.

I began working as an academic librarian in 2007, and in 2008 a colleague asked me to collaborate on a research project. The purpose of the research was to understand how foreign students at our institution perceived and used the library's resources and services. We had a significant number of international students, and I was motivated to participate in this project because the results would help inform my practice as an information literacy librarian. As I pored over the transcripts and survey results, I became amazed at just how different their experiences and expectations of libraries were from my own.

My colleague and I disseminated the results of our research as widely as possible; not only did we present at the Ontario Library Association's annual Super Conference, but to my delight, our research led to international travel as well. We presented at the American Library Association's Annual Conference in Chicago, and we traveled to Hangzhou, China, to attend the Shanghai (Hangzhou) International Library Forum (SILF). At SILF, I had the opportunity to meet Ellen Tise, who was the president of IFLA at the time. Meeting librarians from other countries and visiting libraries around the world kindled my interest in both international librarianship and international volunteering.

Dee Winn, Quebec, Canada

question "What does international librarianship mean to you?" 72 percent of respondents said that it means "participating in international resource sharing" and the same percentage indicated it means "working as a librarian in another country." Other responses included "networking with librarians in person from other countries at library conferences" (71 percent), "connecting online with librarians from other countries" (70 percent), going on a brief library study or tour abroad (46 percent), and sending weeded books to be distributed to developing nations (20 percent). All of these options reflect activities that are typically associated with international librarianship.

When asked, "Do you personally think that international librarianship is an important role for librarians?" 74 percent answered "yes," 21 percent answered that "it depends," and only 1 percent said "no." This finding indicates that the overwhelming majority of librarians believe that IL is an important function of our profession. The number-one response to the question "What ways do you think are the best for learning more about international librarianship?" selected by 85 percent of survey participants, was "participating in some sort of international project or program yourself." We could not agree more, and we believe that of all the various IL activities, participating in an IL volunteer program is the best way to become an international librarian.

Notes

1. Peter Lor, "Critical Reflections on International Librarianship," *Mousaion* 25, no. 1 (2008): 1–15.

2. Stephen J. Parker, "International Librarianship—A Reconnaissance," *Journal of Librarianship* 6, no. 4 (1974): 221.

3. J. Periam Danton, *The Dimensions of Comparative Librarianship* (Chicago: American Library Association, 1973), 52.

4. Peter Lor, "International and Comparative Librarianship: A Thematic Approach," 2010, https://pjlor.files.wordpress.com/2010/07/book-front -matter.pdf.

5. Melanie Sellar, "Strategies for Engaging in International Librarianship: Misconceptions and Opportunities," *SLIS Student Research Journal* 6, nos. 1 and 2 (2016).

6. Discussion lists, American Library Association, 2017, www.ala.org/aboutala/ offices/iro/iroactivities/discussionlists.

7. Ravindra Sharma, ed., *Libraries in the Early 21st Century: An International Perspective* (Boston: De Gruyter Saur, 2012), 1.

8. Libraries Without Borders, 2017, https://www.librarieswithoutborders.org/about-us.

9. Karen Bordonaro, *International Librarianship at Home and Abroad* (Cambridge, MA: Chandos, 2017).

chapter 2

Why? Because the World Needs You

I DON'T KNOW IF ARISTOTLE DID MUCH VOLUNTEER WORK BACK IN the old days, but he is reported to have claimed that the essence of life is to serve others and do good. Fair warning: if you choose to follow Aristotle's wise advice and become an international volunteer, you will have to get used to the following responses from your colleagues, friends, and family, and even from complete strangers:

- Why?
- Don't we have enough problems at home for you to help with?
- You are braver than I!
- Why?
- When do you have the time?
- You do this for free?
- Why?
- Your family lets you do this?
- Isn't that dangerous?
- Why?

When I first began volunteering internationally, I was a bit defensive when others reacted in surprise or confusion, and I would go on and on in great detail defending my work, reassuring concerned family and colleagues, and attempting to convert doubters. I have since learned to just smile and nod, and raise my hands in the air with a "what can I say?" gesture. There are people who will understand what you do and why, there are people who will be interested in your travels and in pursuing similar opportunities, and there are people who will just think you are crazy. If you are reading this chapter, you probably fall into one of the first two categories.

Volunteerism, when conducted with forethought, planning, and expertise, results in a win-win for both the volunteer and the host organization. If you are a student or a practicing or retired information professional who is considering pursuing international volunteerism, rest assured that the benefits are plentiful, and those benefits are both personal and professional.

Personal Benefits

The personal benefits associated with volunteering internationally include a larger worldview, intrinsic rewards, and the opportunity to make the world a better place, to name just a few. Each individual will experience different rewards and will benefit from their journey in ways unique to them.

WORLDVIEW

The *Merriam-Webster Dictionary* defines the term "worldview" as "a comprehensive conception or apprehension of the world especially from a specific standpoint."[1] If a worldview is how one sees life, then traveling (for work or pleasure) expands one's worldview. Through international volunteerism, LIS professionals have an opportunity to travel and experience new cultures, and to see that life is larger and more diverse than the culture experienced in their one small corner of the world. Whether volunteering in Africa, Central America, Asia, or Europe, the volunteer will experience foreign cultures and ways of life. Whether living with a host family, in a rental unit, or in a hotel, volunteers will have the opportunity to become immersed in daily life in another country and all that it entails: cultural and religious rituals, social mores and customs, traditions, and festivals and holidays. International volunteers may be exposed to new languages (such as the twenty-one Mayan dialects spoken throughout Guatemala) whether they speak these languages or not. There may even be various languages spoken within a group of volunteers traveling together. Volunteers will also experience new foods, cooking methods, and mealtime customs, such as dabbawalas delivering hot meals in India. While our world is becoming much more connected, there are still foods that are only available in specific local regions, and international travel affords one the privilege of sampling foreign cuisine on-site.

With this exposure to new sights, sounds, tastes, languages, and practices comes an expanded worldview. Volunteers develop an appreciation for the diversity of our planet, and ideally an appreciation for different ways of life. With exposure and experience, one becomes more accepting of cultures that are foreign, and more interested in trying new things and new experiences. While broadening one's worldview and exposure to other cultures and ways of life through books, movies, the arts, and food is important, there is no substitute for completely immersing oneself in another culture through direct contact. On their return to the familiar, volunteers are more aware and appreciative of the various cultures in their community, and are often more accepting of difference and the need for tolerance. In addition, volunteers may also develop a heightened appreciation for their own customs, traditions, language, and food while immersed in another culture; an awareness of what makes them "Canadian" or "American" or "British," and so on, and an appreciation for the familiar. This Canadian author never feels more Canadian than while traveling and craving poutine, maple syrup, and the smell of a cedar forest or the scent of the ocean mist from "back home." It is also important to note that host libraries and institutions will also benefit from learning about the volunteer's life, culture, and home country. International volunteers often become unintentional ambassadors for their home countries, since those volunteers may be the first or the only person the host has ever met from that country. International volunteerism provides wonderful opportunities to learn and grow from each other, and develop partnerships that serve world peace.

INTRINSIC REWARDS

Volunteerism, in any form, is intrinsically rewarding. While there may be no financial or material reward, there is a feeling of personal satisfaction from having given of one's own time and skills to others in need. There is pride in a job well done, in having shared one's skills, expertise, and experience with other information professionals, making their job easier, their space more inviting or efficient, their collection larger or more organized, or their staff more knowledgeable. While some host organizations want to show their gratitude with gifts or food, or with presentations and crafts from their youngest patrons, many will merely offer a heartfelt thank-you, and that is all that should be expected as an international volunteer. The fact that your presence as a volunteer is necessary speaks to the fact that the host organization needs help without additional cost, and there should be no burden placed on them to provide you with material rewards.

Soliciting donations, traveling to a new locale, exposing yourself to a new culture, and getting to work helping an organization with which you are unfamiliar is a huge accomplishment. It is important to reflect on this. Taking a risk, being self-reliant, and enriching the lives of others are no small feats. Be mindful of what you accomplish each day when volunteering internationally; be thankful for the opportunity, and pat yourself on the back for all that you accomplish, no matter how small. Successfully navigating a new transportation system in a country where you don't speak the language; conducting a story time in Mexico with the constant boom of funeral cannons in the background; ordering lunch when you can't read a menu and don't recognize a single dish; instilling confidence in a library assistant who is afraid of being silly while reading aloud—these are all accomplishments that are unique to international library volunteerism and provide a satisfying sense of achievement that remains long after the adventure.

In Emily Esfahani Smith's book *The Power of Meaning: Crafting a Life That Matters*, the author proposes that people achieve personal happiness through meaning, and by living a meaningful life.[2] Smith states that "meaning" can be defined as connecting and contributing beyond one's own self. She suggests that having a purpose, contributing to society, and serving others are living a meaningful life, and that those who feel their life has meaning are ultimately happier people. By volunteering, one is contributing to and serving others, and thus living a meaningful life.

Are you still not convinced of the power of volunteering? Science has shown that volunteering can have a profoundly positive effect on both one's mental and physical health. An article in the American Psychological Association's journal *Psychology and Aging* "linked volunteerism to lower all-cause mortality among older adults." The article connected volunteerism with "reducing hypertension risk" and "altering the psychological or biological stress response among older adults. Performing volunteer work may give individuals perspective on their own life struggles, promoting more positive coping strategies in the face of potentially stressful situations."[3]

Seeing how others live and work, and getting out of our own heads and our daily grind, can provide clarity and can make our own insurmountable issues seem less important and much easier to overcome. As Mahatma Gandhi said, "The best way to find yourself is to lose yourself in the service of others."[4]

The study entitled "Doing Good Is Good for You" found just what the study's name suggests. The results of the study showed that 75 percent of employees who had volunteered reported feeling happier, and 90 percent reported an improvement in mood. More than 75 percent reported experiencing less stress, and more than 95 percent said that "volunteering enriched their sense of purpose in life" (which, in turn, has been found to strengthen one's immune function).[5] Who would say no to a good mood, reduced stress, lower blood pressure, and living longer?

PAYING IT FORWARD

The friendships formed while volunteering internationally are unique and precious. People who normally would have never met find themselves working side by side, crossing cultural, religious, and language barriers in the pursuit of a common goal. Those volunteers who stay with host families or travel as a group and live together in shared accommodation will see each other at both their best and their worst. Histories and personal and professional anecdotes are shared during downtime and while working together. Volunteers may have to rely on the kindness of the host "strangers" to help them adjust to new surroundings and practices. Mutual trust is formed, and bonds that will last a lifetime. Regardless of whether or not volunteers will ever see their new friends again in person, these friendships are rewarding in and of themselves and are truly unique to the international volunteer experience.

Volunteering your time, money, and expertise to travel a great distance to a library or organization in need is inspiring. Colleagues, family, and friends who may not have previously had the opportunity or interest in volunteering may be stirred to pursue something similar, either at home or abroad. In leading by example and giving back to society, volunteers are serving as models for the younger generation. Volunteers take pride in knowing that they have given altruistically of themselves. International volunteers may also notice that the current phenomenon of "paying it forward," or doing a good deed for someone who then does a good deed for someone else, often occurs as a result of volunteer trips. Those receiving the services of a volunteer or group service trip are often inspired to start local volunteer initiatives and become more civic-minded. International volunteers, overwhelmed by the generosity and gratitude from their hosts, are often moved to donate to local health initiatives in their host country, or to raise awareness back home about the issues they witnessed firsthand while volunteering. On returning home, volunteers may feel compelled to bring attention to any local problems with literacy, poverty, clean water, and health that they encountered while abroad. This "paying it forward" phenomenon is rewarding for not only the volunteer and the recipients, but also for their ever-widening circle of connections. It is rewarding, yes, but this is also how monumental changes occur, starting from one good deed.

Professional Benefits

Research has shown that "those who give their time and effort to others end up achieving more success than those who don't."[6] The Wharton professor Adam Grant has found that "the most successful people in a wide range of jobs are those who focus on contributing to others."[7] Throughout Grant's research and writing, he categorizes workers into either takers, matchers, or givers: takers seek to get as much as possible from others, matchers are in for an even trade, and givers are rare and unique in that they give with no expectation of any return.[8] International volunteers are unique and definitely fall into the givers category. Although volunteers may not expect or desire anything in return for their generosity, the incidental professional rewards of international volunteerism are numerous and comprehensive.

SKILLS: OLD AND NEW

Volunteering internationally gives LIS professionals the opportunity to revisit skills they may no longer use, reinforce skills that may not be necessary in their daily work, and learn new skills. New LIS graduates may be thrust into the role of supporting seasoned staff who are eager for a fresh perspective or for exerting a North American influence. Academic librarians may find themselves providing story times to schoolchildren; cleaning, weeding, and reorganizing shelves and homework help space; or creating and conducting craft programs. These are all skills not usually associated with academic library work, and they may be skills that have been unused for many years. While volunteering in Guatemala, our cataloging team was forced to recall skills they had acquired in library school, since most members of the team now work in information settings with cataloging departments and individual librarians are not required to catalog items in their daily work. In Guatemala, the team worked collectively to navigate cataloging issues and ensure that the system decided upon would be beneficial to the school library after our departure, as well as easy to replicate as new items arrived and other volunteer groups became involved. This process had a significant positive effect on the team's problem-solving skills by the end of the trip.

When traveling as a group or volunteering with others, international volunteers inevitably acquire knowledge from the group itself. Sharing personal and professional stories and working together to come up with solutions to problems and issues on the ground enhance volunteers' ability to function within a team. Volunteers quickly learn how to live and work with a group of strangers from varying backgrounds who have different values, beliefs, and professional practices. Followers and leaders emerge, and volunteers may be surprised by their role within the group; this is very important in terms of self-reflection, self-awareness, and personal growth. While traveling or working with a team, volunteers may notice that their leadership skills improve. Some may be thrust into a project manager role, perhaps tasked with assisting a library transitioning to online borrowing, and those with experience or interest in the area may become the de facto project manager. The skills associated with managing a team, and laying out a project time line, budget, and action items, will all be exercised and strengthened.

Volunteers also often take on a teaching role when assisting internationally, especially when working in school libraries or on literacy initiatives, and they will often experience an increase in related skills. Such skills might include public speaking, empowering others, leading discussions and meetings, training and coaching, and pedagogical decision-making. Sometimes practical decisions regarding functionality are necessary, perhaps assisting an organization with decision-making about instituting external loan privileges, parameters, and rollout. Volunteers who become involved in navigating such decisions and processes will strengthen their own decision-making skills and be able to translate those experiences when they return to their own workplace. While volunteering in Guatemala, both authors were part of a group tasked with finding a (free) solution to missing safety pins. Children visiting the small community lending library were given a lending card featuring the borrower's name, which they pinned onto their clothing while in the library. These pins were costly for the small library and were disappearing daily as mothers in the community used the pins while sewing to make the traditional Mayan clothes that their children wore each day. Our group offered suggestions that included identity cards on a string to be worn around the neck or wrist, or storing the cards at the main desk. This was a beneficial learning opportunity for the group, since it was an issue that required some creativity and problem-solving, and it was an issue that no one in the group had experienced before in the profession.

RELATIONSHIPS

Whether you are working with a team of volunteers or traveling solo, your networks will expand as a result of international volunteership. New friendships are made and professional contacts are acquired around the world. Those within a volunteer group may become future research and writing partners. Professional or institutional partnerships often form, and these partnerships frequently result in future information or personnel exchanges. Some volunteers return annually to the same country or organization, providing long-term assistance and forming strong connections. With these network connections, volunteers, and particularly new graduates looking for work, will increase their opportunities to grow professionally. Those nearing the end of their professional lives may find such strong connections that they decide to relocate to the host country for retirement, continue volunteering on a regular basis, or devote more time to volunteering after their career is complete. Regardless, broadening your LIS network and communicating with professionals around the world keep you current and involved and increase your exposure to new opportunities, ideas, and issues.

Benefits for Those Volunteering Virtually

International volunteers who are able to assist others virtually also experience many rewards. Learning how to effectively communicate across time zones and to overcome language and cultural barriers are valuable skills. The technological skills involved in volunteering remotely, managing virtual applications, and navigating various databases and types of software are highly sought-after skills. Virtual volunteers may also experience an unequal level of information and communication technology between themselves and the host organizations, often referred to as the "digital divide."[9] Learning to compensate for and accommodate any degree of digital divide, and learning to solve problems and be creative, are all valuable skills and professional assets. And as anyone who has conducted virtual and live-chat help

Receiving More Than You Give

THERE ARE MANY reasons why I volunteer internationally. To be honest, I can't imagine that what I've given has been as valuable as what I've received. I've learned how to build, make, and fix things ranging from walls and houses to improvised toys. I've learned to eat what is available and adapt to whatever climate and circumstances I find myself in without complaint. More than anything, I've learned that I don't know much, but the people I meet halfway across the world can teach me a lot. In Zambia, I went to a community of thousands that Google didn't map even though it's only an hour away from Lusaka. I won't pretend that my construction skills wowed my hosts, but I hope the fact that I showed up counts for something.

Sarah Stang, British Columbia, Canada

sessions knows, communicating effectively online is a unique skill. The lack of visual cues, body language, and inflection can make virtual communication very difficult. Through their experience, virtual or remote volunteers will be rewarded with enhanced online communication skills in addition to the technological skills used to virtually assist the host organization; these are both valuable transferable skills in the LIS profession.

Benefits to the Profession

Volunteering internationally also has wider rewards in terms of the profession as a whole. International volunteers serve as advocates and ambassadors for the LIS profession, whether intentionally or unintentionally. In valuing libraries and access to information and reaching out to colleagues

International Volunteering: Go for It

VOLUNTEERING WITH LIBRARIANS Without Borders has been one of the most rewarding and educational experiences of my career. I love public libraries and the role they play in their communities, but my scope and understanding were limited to my experiences here at home (in Los Angeles). I had been working in libraries since I was teenager, but had only been a librarian a few years and was still learning and growing into the role. By working with the Asturias Academy library and its staff, I was able to gain a deeper understanding of the challenges our library colleagues face in countries where educational support and resources are scarce. I gained a new appreciation of the resources I have and am able to provide to my community.

The opportunity to use my skill set to give back and to experience a new environment was priceless. The staff, the children, and my trip mates have all contributed to my growth as a librarian and have inspired me to be more involved in our field and work towards helping all libraries meet the needs of their communities. As library day team leader for my trip, I developed new leadership skills that I use regularly. The trip also provided wonderful mentorship from the trip leaders, who are more experienced librarians and have guided me through important career decisions and opportunities. The experience is one that I will always carry with me and has pushed me to strive to be better and work harder.

Celia Avila, California, U.S.A.

and organizations around the world to create, support, and strengthen other organizations, volunteers are acting as advocates for the value and future of our profession. Using one's own time and money to assist libraries and fellow professionals in need sends a strong message that LIS professionals care and that our work is important and valuable.

Through this service to the profession, volunteers will also return to their regular employment with renewed energy and enthusiasm. Travel, experiencing new cultures, meeting new people, seeing firsthand how other libraries and professionals are operating around the world, and revisiting skills that may have been lost are all facets of international volunteerism that can inspire professionals who may have become bored, disenchanted, or are nearing burnout. Following a volunteer trip, new professionals may find clarity in terms of location or which aspect of LIS work they would like to focus on: public, academic, special, or corporate, to name a few. Those nearing the end of their career may take pride in sharing their accumulated knowledge and expertise with those in need, in a culmination of their life's work, so to speak.

The international volunteer experience can also be shared to the benefit of others in your professional network. Providing professional development (PD) for colleagues is a very rewarding way to share your experience, and will bene-

Raising Awareness

THERE IS NOTHING in the world that can replace the space and resources that a library provides for young, inquisitive minds. My goal is to raise awareness and encourage like-minded individuals to donate money or book resources to the school library I visited in Guatemala. It certainly helps that I have now worked with the school director in person, and I know that he is an innovative and passionate thinker who has great intentions for his community. I'm also a member of my regional library association, the Ontario Library Association. Having led an international volunteer trip, I am now considering developing a proposal for the association's conference.

Jorge Rivera, Ontario, Canada

fit both you and your colleagues. Providing sessions for colleagues or interest groups on the different cultures you experienced, the libraries you visited and their practices, and describing any valuable features that could be translated and adopted in your own organization are all ways of sharing knowledge and expertise. Offering training on serving newcomers from the perspective of a colleague who experienced it firsthand would also be valuable.

Those who are unable or unwilling to volunteer internationally can still share in the experience and gain valuable knowledge through such professional development opportunities, and others may be inspired to volunteer in the future. Volunteers might also choose to conduct further research, publish, or present at a conference. These outputs could be based on the actual

Lasting Impression

EARLY ON IN my career, I attended a very memorable professional development day about serving newcomers. The session was organized by the city of London, Ontario, and included local health professionals, social workers, community leaders, and public library staff. The first half of the day featured a panel of newcomers candidly describing their experiences on coming to Canada, and the programs and services they required and would have benefited from to be successful in their new home. My role was within the public library group, and we were tasked with developing programs and services for newcomers within the library system based on these candid firsthand accounts. I often reflect on that very moving and powerful day, but I was also recently reminded of that session while volunteering on a small island in Central America. I was stranded at the airport on arrival with no phone service, a language barrier, and the prearranged driver nowhere in sight to take me to my accommodation. I had no local change for the pay phone to call my ground contact, there were no available taxis, it was late in the evening, and I was being approached by people trying to take my luggage and usher me into their cars. While I was able to eventually make it to my apartment, in that lonely moment I realized that I was the newcomer; this was another "a-ha" moment for me, however small. I have since shared this experience with other professionals when discussing newcomers in our libraries, and it has affected how I interact with international students at my campus. Having been in their shoes, I am better equipped to sympathize and relate, and am possibly more willing to accommodate them than some colleagues with a smaller worldview.

Cate Carlyle, Nova Scotia, Canada

trip experience, or they could be focused on advocating for global access to information or technology, or on the creation of local groups to fund-raise for the partnership organization, to name just a few possibilities.

The World Needs You

It is clear that the benefits from volunteering internationally are plentiful and unique to each experience or trip. Traveling the world and experiencing new or different aspects of the profession will greatly enhance your worldview and may provide new perspective for those stuck in a rut. Paying it forward and helping others give our lives meaning, which can ultimately increase our happiness quotient. Choosing to give back and to get out of our comfort zones may inspire others to do the same. The opportunity to strengthen skills, try new things, and test our limits both personally and professionally pays off in terms of renewed energy and interest, better health, and a feeling of pride and accomplishment. Sharing this unique experience with others upon your return will widen your network and provide increased opportunities for professional growth, while also enriching and influencing the lives of your colleagues. International volunteers are ambassadors for the profession, acting on their passion for information services and giving of themselves to ensure equal access to information for everyone around the world. They provide advocacy for the profession at a time when it is paramount to the survival of library and information sciences.

Notes

1. *Merriam-Webster Dictionary*, 2017, https://www.merriam-webster.com/dictionary/worldview.
2. Emily Esfahani Smith, *The Power of Meaning: Crafting a Life That Matters* (New York: Crown, 2017).
3. Rodlescia S. Sneed and Sheldon Cohen, "A Prospective Study of Volunteerism and Hypertension Risk in Older Adults," *Psychology and Aging 28*, no. 2 (June 2013): 578–86.
4. M. K. Gandhi Institute for Non-Violence, 2017, www.gandhiinstitute.org/volunteering-internships.
5. "Doing Good Is Good for You," *United Health Group*, 2013, www.unitedhealthgroup.com/~/media/UHG/PDF/2013/UNH-Health-Volunteering-Study.ashx.
6. Arianna Huffington, "Burnout: Time to Abandon a Very Costly Delusion,"

Huffington Post, 2014, www.huffingtonpost.com/arianna-huffington/burnout_b_5102468.html.

7. Adam Grant, "The Secret to Success Is Giving, Not Taking," *Scientific American*, 2013, https://www.scientificamerican.com/article/the-secret-to-success-is-giving-not-taking.

8. Adam Grant, *Give and Take* (New York: Viking, 2013).

9. Joan M. Reitz, "Online Dictionary for Library and Information Science," 2004, www.abc-clio.com/ODLIS/odlis_d.aspx.

The Gift That Keeps on Giving

I'M SURE I could write an entire book on the ways that volunteering internationally has enriched my professional and personal life. However, for your sake, I'll try to keep things brief here. First and foremost, my volunteer experiences in Zambia and Guatemala gave me the invaluable feeling that I was making a difference by giving back and contributing to an important cause that was much greater than myself or my library job. Witnessing firsthand as elementary school students were able to borrow books for the first time because our volunteer work was (and remains) a life-changing experience. Guatemala does not have a reading culture, and not only are there few libraries in the country, but the majority are closed stacks. One of my fondest childhood memories is of the regular trips my family took to our local public library and the excitement of bringing home as many books as I could carry. It is truly an honor to be a librarian and have the opportunity to provide other children with that same privilege.

I have benefited professionally from my volunteer work in ways that have exceeded my wildest dreams. Take the book you're currently holding in your hands—Cate and I volunteered together, kept in touch over the years, and eventually signed a contract to write this book. Cate and I have also presented about international librarianship at the Ontario Library Association's Super Conference, and at British Columbia's annual library conference.

International volunteering really is a life-changing experience. I've collaborated with librarians from numerous countries to improve students' access to information, literacy-based programs, books, and technology. I have visited the homes of local residents to share meals and stories and receive instruction in skilled trades such as weaving and tortilla-making. I've met new friends from around the world, mentored and been mentored, traveled to far-flung places, and I have wonderful memories that will last me throughout my lifetime. I am happy to consider myself a librarian and a global citizen.

Dee Winn, Quebec, Canada

chapter 3

Oh! The Places We've Been . . .

All growth is a leap in the dark, a spontaneous unpremeditated act without benefit of experience. —Henry Miller, 1891–1980

WE ARE TWO LIBRARIANS WHO HAVE HAD THE OPPORTUNITY TO VOLunteer in five different countries in Africa, Central America, and North America. Our main goal in this chapter is to show you that if we can do it, you can too. We would like to share the highlights and unexpected surprises of our adventures and encourage you to pursue your dream of volunteering abroad.

Dee's International Volunteer Trips

Volunteering has been an important part of my life since I was in secondary school. My early experiences volunteering with various local, national, and international organizations (such as Habitat for Humanity) set the stage for my enthusiasm for international volunteering experiences. I traveled to South Africa's acclaimed Kruger National Park not because I was curious about whether hyenas would be able to scale the ten-foot chain-link fence that separated their space from our camping area, but because I wanted to engage in various community development projects in Livingstone, Zambia, and the service trip I chose included tourist stops in South Africa. Likewise, I volunteered in Guatemala not because the trip included free time in Guatemala City and Antigua (an exceptionally charming small city), but because I wanted to be involved in the amazing work being done in Quetzaltenango (Xela). I met amazing people on both trips, learned a lot, and accomplished my goal of giving back to the global community.

MAKING AN IMPACT WITH AFRICAN IMPACT

Way back in the day, when G Adventures was known as Gap Adventures, they offered a Zambia Community Work & Safari Trip. The trip was for two weeks: the first week would be spent volunteering, and the second week would be spent traveling to Botswana and Kruger National Park in South Africa to try and see the "Big Five" (lion, elephant, leopard, Cape buffalo, and black rhinoceros). This combination of volunteer work and leisure sounded like the perfect adventure for me, and I enthusiastically signed up for the trip that began in Livingstone, Zambia.

I worked with fourteen other international volunteers from Austria, Australia, Canada, New Zealand, and the United States to help with various initiatives geared toward community development. This program was unique because we were given the opportunity to participate in different areas of community development each morning and afternoon. As a result, I had the opportunity to teach an HIV/AIDS prevention workshop in a state prison, help organize books in a classroom, run a sports program, provide assistance on a farm, serve meals to homeless senior citizens, help build a new home, and assist with providing medication to people with illnesses who lived in remote areas. We would usually help with one project in the morning, return to the hostel for lunch, and then assist with a different project in the afternoon.

The state prison for men in Livingstone is the only correctional facility I have ever been to, and upon entering the building, what I found most overwhelming was the stench. To this day, I can only describe the smell as a disorienting mixture of offensive odors, and I struggled to adjust to it as the guards quickly escorted us to the room where I would present the workshop. Although my presentation went flawlessly, my worst fears came true. Since the presentation focused on how to lower your chances of acquiring a sexually transmitted disease or HIV by practicing safe sex, I'd anticipated receiving some extremely personal questions from the men that would include descriptions of situations they had encountered. And that is exactly what happened—the inmates asked me a lot of questions; a lot of extremely creative questions that I'm sure were designed to make me blush. Somehow, someway, I managed to keep a professional demeanor at all times, and I responded to their questions in a matter-of-fact way.

One morning I had the opportunity to organize books in a classroom, a project I was particularly excited about because I was working in an education library at the time and was knowledgeable about not only the classics in children's and young adult literature, but the current best-selling books as well. The classroom was a small, cement structure with a few bookshelves on the back wall and a couple of spinners at the far side of the room. I had to unpack boxes of donated books and set them up for display. The most fulfilling part of this work was witnessing the students' enthusiasm and excitement for books—they took them off the shelves and spinners as quickly as I could unpack them.

The most touching project I participated in was a medical outreach initiative. I traveled to remote villages with a young volunteer (a Canadian sec-

Zambia: Quick Facts

ZAMBIA GAINED INDEPENDENCE from the United Kingdom in 1964 and has an estimated population of 15,510,000. It is home to more than seventy different Bantu-speaking ethnic groups, the most numerous of which is the Bemba, who make up approximately 21 percent of the population. When literacy is defined as the ability to read and write English for those fifteen years old or older, the total literacy rate in the country is 63 percent. However, there is a considerable disparity between the literacy rate for men (71 percent) and women (56 percent). Zambia's economy collapsed in the 1970s, when the price of copper, its main export, fell substantially. The economy became stable in the 2000s, due primarily to foreign investment in mining (https://www.cia.gov/library/publications/the-world-factbook/geos/za.html).

ondary school student who wanted to become a doctor) to check in with people who had various illnesses, record their symptoms, and provide them with medication (vitamins and Ibuprofen). Each person we visited apologized to us for not having food to give us and expressed further remorse if they only had one stool outside of their hut (because only one of us could sit down). Among them were people who were dying of HIV/AIDS and other serious illnesses. To this day, one of the happiest people I've ever met in my life was a young man I encountered while doing this work. He lived in a hut and had to use a wheelchair because of a physical disability. We had a wonderful visit with him, and as we left he reminded us that we all have things to be grateful for, and indeed he is right. My experience in Livingstone was life-changing because it was the critical point where I realized I could merge my personal and professional interests. My first international volunteer trip came four years into my career as a librarian, but I would take two more trips in the next four and a half years.

MY CONNECTION TO LIBRARIANS WITHOUT BORDERS

By the time I participated on my first Librarians Without Borders (LWB) service trip, I had wanted to become actively engaged in the organization for years. I started working on my MLIS degree at the University of Western Ontario (UWO) shortly after some former UWO students had created LWB. It wouldn't be an overstatement to say that there was a strong buzz around the North Campus Building about LWB and all the amazing things it was sure to accomplish, and I instinctively knew that I would become involved with this organization. I was one of the lucky few MLIS graduates who had secured employment in a tenure-track position before the end of my final semester. I officially graduated in April and began working as an information literacy librarian in July. What did I do with all the passion I felt towards LWB? Well, I put it on the back burner and didn't give it another thought for seven and a half years, when an e-mail I received via a librarians' discussion list caught my eye. At the time, I was working at the University of British Columbia (UBC), and students at the School of Library, Archival and Information Studies had decided to open a UBC student chapter of LWB. One of my colleagues had sent the e-mail, asking librarians to contact her if they were interested in becoming the committee advisor for UBC's new LWB student chapter. The primary responsibilities for this role were to serve as a liaison between the student chapter and LWB's Executive Committee and to provide mentorship, advice, and assistance to the student chapter. I instantly recognized this as the special invitation I had been waiting for—this was my opportunity to finally become involved with LWB, and very quickly, I made up for all the time I had wasted between wanting to get involved and actually getting involved.

ON GOING TO GUATEMALA

You may think that once you've committed to the decision to go on an international volunteer trip, have applied to (if necessary) and been accepted in a program, and have checked off every single one of the million action items on your pre-trip to-do list, that you would be 100 percent ready for the trip. But let me tell you about the biggest curveball that was thrown my way on my first LWB trip—I literally didn't see it coming. Although it was months before the trip, I essentially felt that everything was good to go. I was extremely excited about traveling to Guatemala to volunteer at the Asturias Academy; after all, it had been more than ten years since I had become one of LWB's biggest fans. I had been asked to be a member of the Cataloging Team and was informed that training was going to take place as part of our pre-trip preparation. I was a bit nervous about cataloging because I hadn't done any beyond what I'd completed for a cataloging course in the first semester of library school, but I was eager to help out any way that I could. And then the Big Ask came—the service trip leader and a few other LWB Executive Committee members asked me if I would be the Cataloging Team's leader for the trip. Now, I was ready and eager (though not an all-star cataloger) to be a member of the team, but actually being responsible for the work of the team in a language that I don't read, write, or speak? That was just too much! I asked for some time to think about their request and spent way too much time mulling it over.

I didn't know what to do. I had recently completed a term as the acting head at the University of British Columbia's Education Library and had really enjoyed it. In fact, that experience confirmed my suspicion that I would enjoy managing people, and it eventually led me to seek out another position as a manager. But managing volunteers—people who paid a lot of money to then work for free? Thankfully, the LWB Executive Committee members showed me the cataloging manual and procedure and, after realizing that I could handle it, I decided to accept the additional responsibility of leading the Cataloging Team. At that point, the only two things I was a bit worried about were how I would motivate the members of the Cataloging Team (and ensure that they had fun) and who my roommate would be (my fingers were crossed that she wouldn't snore).

The trip always begins in Guatemala City (usually on a Saturday in late April), and the volunteers and trip leader(s) are picked up at the airport and brought to a nearby hostel as they arrive. The group leaves early the next morning to travel (by van) to Xela, and even though it is only 200 kilometers away, it takes quite a few hours to get there. Upon arrival, the group spends some time settling into their rooms, and then they prepare their materials to begin volunteering at Asturias the next day. When volunteers are accepted, they are informed which team they've been placed on. A lot of time is spent matching each volunteer's skills and experiences to the most appropriate team.

Guatemala: Quick Facts

LWB'S GUATEMALA SERVICE TRIP is well established, since it has been running annually for nearly ten years. Guatemala had once been the center of the Maya civilization, but was colonized by the Spanish in the sixteenth century. Guatemala gained independence in 1821, and was ruled by a succession of dictators thereafter. The country experienced a protracted civil war that lasted from 1960 to 1996. The population is estimated to be 15,190,000 and includes a variety of ethnic groups such as mestizos, K'iche', Kaqchikel, Mam, O'eqchi, and other Mayans. The literacy rate is defined as people fifteen years of age and older who can read and write. Though the overall literacy rate is 81 percent, the literacy rate for men is 87 percent and the rate for women is 76 percent. Guatemala's agricultural sector drives its economy and its key exports are sugar, coffee, bananas, and vegetables (https://www.cia.gov/library/publications/the-world-factbook/geos/gt.html).

This trip had three teams: cataloging, communications, and programming. The Cataloging Team was responsible for cataloging the books (they finished cataloging 535 of them). The Communications Team wrote blog posts about our activities, solicited other volunteers to write posts as well, and posted to LWB's social media accounts. The Programming Team's main task was to hold an event known as Library Day. Library Day features unique, age-appropriate library-related activities for each grade level. The activities could include story times, puppet shows, skits, plays, games, and any other activities the team has planned. One of the highlights of this trip was that a circulation system was implemented, so that students were able to take books home for the first time!

We spent the week (Monday-Friday) in Xela, worked at the Miguel Angel Asturias Academy from 8:30 a.m. to 12:30 p.m. each day, had a lunch break, and enjoyed different excursions in the afternoon. Our excursions were a blend of cultural experiences and typical tourist attractions, and included a visit to a local family's home, a visit to a women's textile cooperative, a tour of the Municipal Library, a trip to Fuentes Georginas (hot springs), a soccer game, and a hike at La Muela.

After finishing our work at Asturias, we traveled to San Gaspar Chajul, a remote village located in the mountainous Western Highlands. Librarians Without Borders was exploring the possibility of a new partnership with Limitless Horizons Ixil (LHI). As LWB's first (and only) volunteer group to travel to Chajul, we had the opportunity to meet with LHI staff and librarians to discuss literacy and outreach strategies, provide programming for local children, and visit families in their homes. Our primary goal was to do the groundwork to develop and maintain a new, mutually beneficial relationship between LWB and LHI, and I believe we accomplished that goal.

After spending a few days in Chajul, the group traveled to Antigua for the final day of the service trip. Although we didn't arrive until the late afternoon, we were able to see a few of the main tourist attractions, including the Arco de Santa Catalina, Central Park Plaza, Iglesia de la Merced, and the Church of San Francisco. Early the next morning, I took a shuttle bus with a few other volunteers to the Guatemala City airport. I had met many amazing people from different countries, accomplished a lot of good work, greatly increased my knowledge of Guatemala's history and culture, and had a lot of fun. As I boarded the plane that would take me home to Vancouver, I intuitively knew that I would return to Guatemala. Oh, and in case you were wondering, being the Cataloging Team leader was no big deal and greatly contributed to my overall sense of accomplishment during the trip.

ON GOING TO GUATEMALA . . . AGAIN

On my second trip with LWB, I didn't wait for the Big Ask; instead I submitted an application to be a co-trip leader well before the deadline. I had given it quite a bit of thought since the 2014 trip, and I realized that I wanted to step up to the plate and assume more responsibility the next time I participated on this trip. The co-trip leaders are responsible for liaising with LWB's program director and Asturias Academy's director to decide which projects will be undertaken; recruiting, selecting, training, and preparing all volunteers; and planning the itinerary. My co-trip leader was also LWB's program director and had already established a strong, positive rapport with Asturias' director that led him to trust our leadership. Since the most recent previous trips had different leaders, the volunteers had participated in and visited different places, so my co-trip leader and I were able to plan an itinerary that featured the highlights of each of our previous trips and included many excursions. For starters, upon arriving at our hostel in Guatemala City, we divided into groups based on the attractions we wanted to see: some people went to the zoo, others to the botanical garden, and others just walked around, happy to stretch their legs after long flights. The next day, we spent the morning in a popular square downtown, visited the Union Church of Guatemala, and happened upon a fair in the square. Before making our way to Xela (home of the Asturias Academy), we stopped by Piedra Santa, a publisher, bookstore, and educational center, in order to purchase books for Asturias' library.

Once we arrived in Xela, there were a few more trips. The first was a visit to a public library operated by the Bank of Guatemala. Even though the books there are accessible on shelves, they are closed stacks and patrons must ask the librarian to retrieve the books for them. The books can only be used in the library and cannot be borrowed. From the library, we walked a short distance to El Calvario Cementerio, a cemetery renowned for its colorful monuments and eclectic style. We learned about the local legend of the star-crossed lovers Vanushka and Javier and listened with rapt attention as our tour guide shared his memories of hiding from soldiers, behind tombs, on his way to elementary school during the country's civil war. Other trips we made from Xela were to a women's textile co-op and to a glassblowing co-op in Cantel. Once we had finished working at the Asturias Academy, we traveled to Panajachel. This small town is located on the shore of Lake Atitlán, and seeing this famous lake was a highlight of the trip for many of us. We stayed overnight in Panajachel, which gave the volunteers an opportunity to visit other islands surrounding the lake, but we all met up for dinner and karaoke in the evening. From Panajachel we traveled to Antigua and stayed in a lovely hostel called El Hostal before traveling home the next day.

Lessons Learned

- Whenever you have the opportunity to step out of your comfort zone, take it.
- International volunteering is a life-changing, educational experience.
- You will learn as much about yourself as you do about the new countries, people, and situations you experience.
- Coca-Cola in Guatemala tastes sweeter than it does in the United States and Canada.

Cate's International Volunteer Trips

I too have volunteered on three separate international library trips, in addition to my regular volunteer work at home, which involves book festivals; library outreach at festivals, shelters, and missions; student and children's events; literacy and reading workshops and presentations; and library fund-raising and advocacy initiatives. My international volunteer work has included an organized service trip, a trip that I arranged, and a trip that was a combination of both. Although it was for a research trip funded by an institutional grant, I have also visited and researched libraries in Oaxaca, Mexico, that are part of the Libros para Pueblos nonprofit organization (an incredible group that creates and supports libraries in schools and communities). I have been fortunate enough to volunteer in Guatemala, Honduras, and Nicaragua, and I hope that I have only just begun.

THE TRIP THAT CHANGED MY LIFE

While working in an academic second language library at a mid-sized university, I was part of a team that went frequently on international trips to promote our academic programs and recruit international students. In my role as librarian for international postsecondary students, I was not required to travel, and I was quite envious of my coworkers' stories about their exotic experiences and regular travels to Asia, Central America, and the Middle East. I came across an interesting e-mail one typical working day when I was feeling quite trapped and bored with my predictable routine; one of those increasingly frequent days when my forties were whizzing by and I was feeling that I had stalled professionally. The e-mail was a call from Librarians Without Borders for LIS professionals and students to apply for its annual service trip to Guatemala. Was this a sign from the heavens? I consulted with my spouse that night and filled out the application, all totally out of character for me (a mom of two who is working full-time, with mounting credit card bills and very little vacation time, does not do such things!). The fact that my family would be lucky enough to attend a royal garden party at Buckingham Palace with the queen of England a scant two weeks after the LWB Guatemala trip made it a bit of a tough sell in terms of finances, timing, and taking time off from work, but I took a leap of faith to do both (no one turns down an invite from the queen). The Guatemala service trip seemed like the answer to my need for meaning, adventure, inspiration, and a new professional challenge, and so I jumped in feet first, completely terrified.

In typical librarian fashion, I researched the socks off of LWB, its previous service trips, and Guatemala. I quickly became aware that Guatemala, a country never before in my lexicon, was not the safest place to travel and doubly so for women. When my father found out about my plans, I received quite a few e-mails from him asking me to reconsider, quoting crime statistics for the country and describing the brutal civil war from which its people were still recovering. Wary but still committed, I researched Guatemalan vaccination requirements and the country's climate, culture, and living conditions. I researched LWB's mission, the libraries they visit, the LWB executive members, and past trips. I consulted open Flickr and Facebook pages for photos from past participants, blog postings, and journal articles. The more I researched, the more I was reassured that LWB's highly structured repeat service trips would be the best option for my introduction into international volunteerism. It may have been mine, but it wasn't LWB's "first rodeo."

Since my application for the trip had been somewhat impulsive, and I struggled to come up with the required fee and plane fare, I chose to fundraise online. My friends and family donated funds, and this enabled me to purchase book and material donations to take with me to Guatemala. I was also informed pre-trip that I would be on the Cataloging Team and was required to attend virtual training sessions with mock cataloging exercises prior to departure. Serendipitously I met Dee, my coauthor on this book, who was also on the Cataloging Team. Dee and I were two of a few Canadians on our service trip, and we kept in touch after the trip. You never know how your life will change and who will come into your life; as I look back now, it is clear that meeting Dee was the first life-changing aspect of that trip for me.

While Dee has described the trip's activities, locales, and duties in detail, I think it is important to add the personal takeaways from my first international volunteer trip, the classic "do as I say, not as I do." Having never been to summer or sleep-away camp, I can only assume that my experience with shared accommodations on the LWB trip was somewhat similar. As we traveled between Guatemala City, Xela, Chajul, and Antigua, the group stayed in hostels, rental accommodations, and in a Catholic retreat. For the most part, volunteers bunked with the same partner or group at each location. Some common concerns included snoring, sleep habits (early/late lights-out preferences), differing personalities, illness, and cleanliness/messiness, all to be expected when rooming with strangers. Another life-changing experience for me occurred within the first few days of the trip while I was journaling in my room. It was mid-morning when I heard a low mechanical hum, and the bed I was sitting on began to shake and the mango on the table beside me rolled off onto the floor. Since the halls were cleaned each day, I assumed it was a particularly loud floor polisher and waited until it passed. It was not until later that day, when the director of the school we were visiting asked if anyone had felt the earthquake that morning, that I realized what had occurred! As a librarian from rural Canada, I believe it best that I was so naive in the moment and did not realize what was happening and therefore didn't panic. This earthquake was life-changer number two; I would forever be much more cognizant of my surroundings and any unusual noise or activity.

As Dee mentioned, we were the first and only LWB group to visit a very remote community library in Chajul, an area hard hit by the civil war and a community reluctant to trust or engage with outsiders. Chajul's remoteness necessitated a somewhat terrifying trip through mountains and on precarious cliffside winding roads. Many in our group succumbed to carsickness, and window seats were at a premium. Chajul itself receives help from many nongovernmental organizations (including the U.S. Peace Corps) and from international charitable and service groups that have offices, temporary workers, and volunteers in the small town. I was struck by the primitive local water supply and housing, the lovely people in their hand-sewn traditional Mayan attire, and the pervasiveness of the smoke from open-fire kitchen areas. We were given a tour of the town, were welcomed into homes, and were treated to local traditional dishes and weaving lessons. With participants in our group from Ireland, Spain, the United States, and Canada, our skin, hair color, and clothing were a point of interest to the locals. There was definitely a bit of culture shock once again for me on arrival in this special town. When others ask why I volunteer internationally when Canada has its own problems, I describe some of the extremes I witnessed in Chajul and reiterate the fact that other areas of the world do not have the basic amenities, services, privileges, freedoms, and rights we sometimes take for granted in North America; our time and efforts are very much needed elsewhere too.

Our work at the community library in Chajul included discussion of the best free open-source software for possible future electronic circulation, and we also provided library programming ideas and conducted sessions for the local schoolchildren. The library staff specifically requested a town hall–like "Q and A" session with us wherein they could ask our team for practical advice about issues in the library. One question that has stuck with me came from a young male library assistant who was in possession of a donated clown suit and oversized shoes for use in story times and festivals. This staffer wanted advice on how to be "silly" with the schoolchildren while making use of the costume and how best to engage them with the stories he was reading. Since no one in our group spoke the specific Mayan dialect of the region, we engaged in a group conversation through an interpreter, and with many gestures and sketches on the whiteboard, we offered ways in which he could engage the children with stories and we demonstrated the actions and movements of a typical clown. This was a third and somewhat surreal life-changing moment in which I was struck by the fact that, even in such a remote and unique area of the world, LIS issues such as encouraging engagement during story time, crowd control, and developing confidence while reading aloud are common concerns.

At the end of our stay in Xela, the director of the school housing the library we had been working in invited us to a meal and social gathering in thanks for our work at the library. We were treated to a large buffet of local foods prepared by the school and library staff and families, as well as a student demonstration of local dances. Attending this event, which I assumed had taken a lot of time, effort, and money to prepare, made me somewhat uncomfortable. I realized that in working with the staff and students, I had felt that we were working side by side as a team whose members were all committed to literacy, education, and bettering the life of the students, and not as a group of outsiders existing on some other level who required thanks and rewards. I had become less aware of our differences and more aware of our commonalities both professionally and personally. This was life-changing moment number four; we are all people first, making our way in this world, trying to help our children and ensure a better life for all. This first trip removed any possibility of an "us versus them" or a "helper versus helpee" mindset for me when volunteering, and it solidified my commitment to volunteering whenever and wherever I could.

GOING SOLO, SORT OF

Having been bit by the international volunteering bug, I was eager for another opportunity to help, and my second trip took me to the Sand Castle community library on the island of Roatan in Honduras. The university where I work has an informal partnership with Partners in Education Roatan (PIER), the nongovernmental organization that runs the Sand Castle Library. A committed and inspiring American expatriate couple founded PIER, and they provide training for local teachers, as well as two bookmobiles which travel from the library to local schools. While chatting with a professor at my university who has provided teacher training for the organization, she mentioned that the library could use assistance on-site, donations, and some informal training for the main library staffer. With her reassurance that most locals spoke English, since I am not fluent in the local language and would be going solo, I went out on a limb and arranged my own volunteer trip to Honduras. I put the word out to a few professionals in my network who were seasoned volunteers and two asked to join my trip. I am a realist, a list maker, and a planner who always makes sure that all "boxes are checked and double-checked," but I was surprised by the depth of planning required for such trips and the many things that might not go according to plan. LWB had spoiled me.

I liaised with the nonprofit and the librarian on the island via e-mail prior to my trip, and I also started following their website and social media accounts. I prepared by ascertaining the best month for my trip, avoiding the rainy season and the weeks when the librarian was off and school was out, as well as selecting a period when my university was not busy. I also started a conversation about what the organization wanted me to do and to bring. The librarian provided a long list of needed supplies, and I fundraised to purchase and bring those supplies with me in extra luggage. I also notified her that I was unable to bring all that was requested; bleach for a "slime" science program was not something I wanted to bring in my luggage! The head of the organization requested that I work with the librarian (a term used without regard to any formal training or academic certification) and help her to improve her LIS knowledge and confidence. After consulting with the professor who had been to the island in the past, I arranged to rent an apartment which was a short beach walk to the library, and I looked into purchasing tickets for the four flights required to get to the island. With boxes checked, and lists being completed, I began to run into a few snags. The professionals who had committed to come with me, share the apartment, and provide supplies were forced to back out due to work commitments at home. The head of the organization also notified me that we would have to change the time for my visit because school would be out and no students or teachers would be at the library. The boxes of Spanish children's books I had ordered online to be delivered directly to the island also briefly went astray. Knowing how important it is to be flexible and to "roll with the punches" when volunteering internationally, I adjusted the date of my travel and enlisted the assistance of my adult daughter, who works part-time in an academic library, to travel with me and help to transport supplies.

Once on the ground in Honduras and settled into our apartment, we delivered the supplies to the head of the organization on the first morning, only to be informed that the library had recently been broken into and the computers stolen. The librarian was also busy trying to set up the library for the coming year after a recent school closure, and the somewhat primitive yet charming building (a former dive facility for tourists) and library collection were in a state of disarray; geckos, bugs, and various rodents had taken refuge in the library over the break. My daughter and I chose to work at Sand Castle from 9:00 a.m. to 5:00 p.m. each day cleaning the shelves, sweeping and sorting, and encouraging the librarian to remove damaged and moldy books. Mold is a common LIS issue, and we had to gently push the librarian to discard both moldy and outdated, factually incorrect items; this is often a tough sell when the collection is very small to begin with. We created a simple classification system, labeled materials, created displays, and tidied and organized the teen and children's areas. We demonstrated the benefits of placing items covers out whenever possible and creating interactive displays that related to the local curriculum. On request, I conducted an informal professional development session for the younger library staff who liaise with schools. I demonstrated how to conduct book talks and how to engage children in story times, and I provided sample programs and activities to encourage literacy. I also worked one-on-one with a few of the staffers who were creating educational games and literacy activities for their school visits.

This volunteer trip was very physical, since we were assisting with opening the library for the year, but it was also very rewarding. Since we were a tiny team of two, we worked hard each day to try and complete our duties in a short time, in very humid conditions with rampant mosquitoes and a stray dog wandering the facility. The fact that the rainy season ran long, destroying the piping and water supply to our apartment, proved challenging, as did the lack of Internet access and time for any sightseeing or social activities after work. Since our apartment did not have reliable Wi-Fi or a TV (or a working toilet after the second day) and the sun set quite early, there was plenty of time for sleep after hours of physical labor in the hot library. Since this was the first trip I had organized myself, I was quite proud of what we accomplished and I took note of a few lessons learned.

A BIT OF BOTH WORLDS

My third service trip took me to Nicaragua (despite the e-mails from my father asking me to reconsider). This trip was arranged once again through an established nonprofit library organization, but with leeway provided to customize the experience and duties. Go for Hope, the American nonprofit organization running the service trips, is committed to providing funding and resources for community-based libraries in Nicaragua. Nicaragua is the second-poorest country in the Americas and its people struggle with poverty, elevated school dropout levels, and incidences of child labor. While in school, children are encouraged to read academic texts, but pleasure reading is not a part of Nicaraguan culture.

The service trip I participated in was to the island of Ometepe, which is located in a large freshwater lake. The island was formed from two volcanoes, Concepción and Maderas, with Concepción still currently active. Ometepe suffered from record rains, floods, and

Lessons Learned

- There is no such thing as too much preparation.
- Always have a backup plan, and extra resources and supplies.
- Make sure you or a fellow traveler speak the language. If not, arrange for an interpreter.
- Print off and bring any online materials you will need because Internet access may not be available or reliable on-site.
- Mother Nature is very unpredictable.
- Gecko wrangling and their removal from your sleeping area is a useful skill.

landslides triggered by the Concepción volcano in 2014, and its people are still recovering. Our trip consisted of our arrival in Managua, the capital city, and then a half day of transport via primitive ferry out to the island and ultimately to a very rural beach community. While in Ometepe, we visited a few community schools and took part in local activities that focused on educating us about the island's culture, traditions, geography, and crops. Group members were divided among homestays in pairs and came together for trips to the schools, activities, and to prepare programming for our school visits.

Our homestays were located in a "citadel" community in the shadow of Concepción that had houses, electricity, water, a health office, and a church, all created by the government for families who had lost their homes during the landslide. The homes were basic concrete dwellings with open-fire, dirt-floor kitchens, electricity, and simple plumbing. The rooms had only sheets for doors, the windows were openings in the concrete, and the bathrooms did not feature a door or a sink (you get to know your homestay family quite quickly in such intimate lodgings). No one in the community spoke English, but there was a hired guide who transported us on our volunteer trips, translated, and also served as a cultural guide helping us to navigate local customs and practices. It was interesting to learn that not all the locals were happy with their new, more modern homes and that, if given the choice, some com-

APR 2 5 2005

Nicaragua: Quick Facts

IN NICARAGUA, ONLY 51 out of 100 children who start the first grade will complete fifth grade, and the average Nicaraguan adult aged 25–40 typically has only 4.6 years of formal schooling. Nicaragua spends $62 per year per student, whereas the United States spends an average of $10,600 per year per student. Both lack of training and very low pay prompt many Nicaraguan teachers to abandon their profession.[1] While children are expected to attend school until the age of 12, UNICEF estimates that 500,000 Nicaraguan children aged 3 to 17 are not in the educational system. Nicaraguan business leaders also suggest that there are between 250,000 and 320,000 child workers, with one in three of these under the age of fourteen.[2]

munity members would have preferred to have stayed in their much simpler (yet unsafe) former community without plumbing or electricity. Elders also informed us that they were beginning to experience some difficulties with disengaged youth who were starting to rebel, and they were in need of someone to volunteer as a town psychologist. Volunteers from various countries were prevalent in the community, helping to build a new church and donating items such as bicycles, but there was no psychologist as of yet. While there was no Wi-Fi in the community, it was possible for some in our group to intermittently gain access using cell phone data, and many of the local youth had cell phones with plans. As an outsider, I was curious as to whether this virtual connection to a vastly different outside world was playing a role in the difficulties among the youth, but I did not find an appropriate opportunity to pursue this question further.

My partner and I were placed in a home with an older couple which also housed their daughter and her two children during the day while their son-in-law fished. Though we spoke only rudimentary Spanish and the family spoke no English, we were able to communicate with the help of gestures, drawings, and an English-Spanish dictionary. Since we were out most days in

SEP 0 4 2007

Mamones

OUR HOMESTAY FAMILY liked to pick *mamones* for us to eat off of their tree. Once peeled, these small, tangy fruits had a very unique texture reminiscent of their nickname, "eyeball fruit." We were also informed that mamones indelibly stained clothing black if dripped. Politely accepting the generosity of our homestay family, I tried a few mamones but quickly found I was unable to stomach this unique snack. I became quite adept at pretending to eat these "eyeballs" while palming them to give to the children later. I am not sure if it was the threat of staining my limited wardrobe or the "eyeball" moniker that affected my ability to enjoy the fruit; it was probably a combination of the two. The prolific Nicaraguan mangoes were another story altogether; I could gladly subsist solely on a diet of the fresh juicy mangoes that lined every street. Such a treat!

Cate Carlyle, Nova Scotia, Canada

service, we interacted with the family in the evening and colored and drew with the children, learning new Spanish words and games, so that the adults could have some free time to themselves. I also tried to make a point of modeling pleasure reading in front of the family and their young children. We became very close to our homestay family despite the language and cultural barriers, and it was an emotional goodbye at the end of our trip.

While there were plans to visit various school libraries in our area, there was a breakdown in communication and we arrived to find that those schools were not open. The closest school arranged to bring the students back to class for a day, although the school was closed for a break, but the school did not have a library (a testament to those young students who did not begrudge coming back to school although it was not in session). We visited the school via horseback and our group delivered supplies, offered programming on creating chessboards and teaching chess as requested by the teacher, and interacted with the students in the classroom and outdoors. Another school we visited was in an extremely remote community that could only be accessed by a forty-minute drive in a rental van and then an hour-long hike through the muddy jungle (my shoes did not make it back alive, and a kindly farmer offered me his rubber boots). The teacher hiked with us, her daily commute, and brought a branch bearing fish she had caught that morning for our lunch. The one-room concrete school had been built two years earlier, served 25 homes in a community of 200, and did not have a library. The students were very timid and apprehensive about our group because they were unaccustomed to outside visitors, and interacting with them proved challenging. We played social circle games with the students, delivered supplies, and worked on a board-game craft activity that was designed for all of the ages represented at the school (primary to teenagers). It was interesting to note that this extremely remote school had an Internet connection and had interacted online with other volunteer groups in North America.

The schools we visited in Ometepe were each staffed by middle-aged female teachers whose dedication to their students and their community was awe-inspiring. The teachers walked to work in all conditions, and worked in very simple surroundings with limited supplies for low wages. It was evident that the students respected and loved these women. Near the end of our trip, back on the mainland, we visited the San Juan del Sur Biblioteca; the first community library in Nicaragua, it was created and is run by another inspiring woman, the American expatriate Jane Mirandette. Since founding the library, Mirandette has also introduced a mobile project that visits more than thirty-four communities, and she has pioneered a "Library in a Box" program that serves dozens of lending programs throughout Central America and Peru. Mirandette's passion for libraries and the Nicaraguan people was evident as she described the collection, the bookmobile, her teams of volunteers, and programming for special needs patrons.

The Ometepe service trip was not as library-focused as I had hoped, so my background as a teacher and school librarian was helpful. That being said, our guide was always diligent in trying to arrange visits to libraries and volunteer opportunities to replace the ones that had fallen through, as well as cultural excursions to teach us about Nicaragua's society and ecology. I am always in awe of the level of passion and commitment that these volunteer organizers and organization founders have; they dedicate their lives to those less fortunate and are always eager to educate those of us embarking on the volunteer journey. While our plans to volunteer in Ometepe's school libraries did not happen as planned, and there were a number of other unforeseen issues with housing and activities (including the six-hour closure of a road in Masaya for a parade when it was the only road that could get us to our next location), the trip was another very important learning experience. I was again reminded of the importance of flexibility when visiting new locales, accommodating differing personalities and habits when traveling as a group (I was proud to once again be the only person not to fall ill), and being prepared with programs, supplies, and activities that could be utilized when the best-laid plans went out the window. Nicaragua is a visually stunning country and the people are genuine, caring, hard-working, and incredibly stoic in the face of adversity. They inspired my partner and me to rededicate ourselves to being mindful of all that is good in the world and to remain committed to ensuring education, access to information, and safe and healthy living conditions for all regardless of their place of birth.

"The Opinions Expressed Here . . ."

Our "notes from the field" are our stories, subjectively told and always 20/20 in hindsight. We have grown and learned from our volunteer work, from each trip and activity. Those who have volunteered with us may have different recollections or takeaways, but it is our hope that our personal stories inspire others to begin the journey and gather their own stories, memories, friends, and experiences. The world is waiting; make a difference.

Notes

1. Go for Hope, 2014, www.goforhope.org/2014/07/23/community-library -projects/.
2. Nina Lakhani, "Poverty in Nicaragua Drives Children Out of School and into the Workplace," *The Guardian*, 2015, https://www.theguardian.com/global -development/2015/may/19/poverty-nicaragua-children-school-education -child-labour.

chapter 4

Get Ready, Get Set, Go

IF YOU HAVE MADE THE DECISION TO VOLUNTEER IN AN INTERNA-tional library, but have no idea where to begin, then congratulations—you are in the right place. This chapter describes the steps you need to take to begin planning your adventure, and it is chock full of useful information that will help you get to wherever it is you want to go. You'll learn how to locate trip opportunities, about the selection process for organized service trips, fund-raising possibilities, which questions to ask your trip organizers (if you take an organized service trip), which items to pack, and much, much more. The first thing you need to know is that there are four different types of international volunteer trips for the solo traveler, and only you can decide which option best meets your expectations and goals. Your first alternative is to participate in an organized service trip; your second choice is to do it yourself and design your own itinerary; and your third option is a structured trip that blends the two previous types. Your final option is to participate in a group trip and volunteer with friends, family, colleagues, or any other group that you're a member of. Now let's see what else there is to know.

Types of Volunteering

An organized service trip is the type of trip where the volunteer pays a fee to an organization and the organization plans every aspect of the trip. Since the organizations that manage these trips make most of the arrangements, the only things you have to do are pay the program fee, book your flight, and show up ready to work. The program fee typically includes some combination (or all) of the following: airport pickup and transportation to your accommodation, accommodation and transportation once you are on-site, meals, cultural and educational or tourist excursions, training materials, and a small donation to the local partner.

There are many advantages to taking part in an organized service trip; the biggest one is that it saves you an enormous amount of time because you don't need to research all of the minute details of the trip, such as making local arrangements for accommodations, the projects you'll participate in, and your transportation needs. The second major advantage is that you'll likely receive project updates and any required training before the trip. You'll have plenty of time to ensure that you fully understand your specific role on the project(s) you'll be involved with. A final benefit to this type of trip is the cohort of like-minded volunteers with whom you will have shared this amazing experience. During the trip, you'll work, eat, laugh, cry, and travel together—and you may even form friendships with people you otherwise would have never met. The major disadvantage of organized service trips is that their program fees can be expensive, and even prohibitive to some. Although you receive a lot of benefits, the fee can be so steep that some people wonder why they need to pay so much money to go somewhere to work for free.

If an organized service trip doesn't appeal to you, you may prefer the do-it-yourself option. The DIY option is exactly what it sounds like—you assume the responsibility for planning every aspect of your trip. It is the exact opposite of the organized service trip because you have full control over every aspect of your trip, and so you will need to research and plan it before you arrive in your chosen country. This includes deciding on a location, contacting local organizations to coordinate your project work, and arranging all of your accommodation and transportation needs yourself. By far, the best advantage of this approach is the flexibility it provides. If your dream is to volunteer in a school library in a favela in Rio de Janeiro on week-days and spend your weekends lounging on Copacabana Beach, then you can make it happen (okay, we admit, that's our dream). Nothing is holding you back from choosing the country you would like to volunteer in, deciding on the duration of your trip, and making sure the trip's expenses match your available funds. The main disadvantage to the DIY trip is that you may not have anyone on the ground to help you if you need emergency assistance.

The structured trip is a perfect combination of the first two options. Structured trips allow you the freedom to choose your location and plan your own travel, but someone else coordinates the project work you'll partic-ipate in. You'll pay a fee to an organization, and they'll typically provide you with a placement, accommodations, and a brief orientation. For the most part, that is where their support ends, and it'll be up to you to work out the details of your volunteer work and arrange your transportation, meals, and other services.

Our advice is that if you are traveling internationally for the first time and don't speak the language of the country you are visiting, you may want to participate in an organized trip before striking out on your own. The train-ing and support that are provided throughout the program will increase your odds of having a successful trip. Once you become an experienced interna-tional traveler, it may prove even more personally rewarding if you volunteer on a structured trip, and then design your own experience. We have had positive experiences with organized, DIY, and structured international vol-unteer trips.

Group trips are a good option for people who want to volunteer with their friends, family, and colleagues. Although its volunteer projects are not library-based, Projects Abroad is an example of an organization that offers groups of five people or more the opportunity to design customized volun-teer trips (https://www.projects-abroad.ca/volunteer-projects/tailor-made -group-trips/).

FIRST STEPS

One good place to begin your search for an organized service trip is chapter 8 of this guide. We have compiled a list of service trips and included brief descriptions of each one. We've also included a separate list of organizations, some of which have volunteer programs. If you need more information, or plan to design your own trip, then Google is the best place to begin your search. One important decision you'll have to make concerns the duration of your trip. You will have to determine how much time you can dedicate to this project. From our experience, projects that last from 1 to 4 weeks are classified as short-term, those that last from 1 to 6 months are considered medium-term, and projects with durations longer than 6 months are considered long-term. Although volunteer opportunities exist around the world, the majority of them are in Africa, Asia, and Central America.

THE APPLICATION/SELECTION PROCESS

The deadline to apply for a spot on an organized service trip is usually three to four months before the trip starts. You can usually find all of the information you need regarding the trip on the organization's website, as well as a name and contact information if you have any questions. Some organizations will hold an information session webinar before the deadline and encourage all interested participants to attend. If you've ever applied to a postsecondary institution for a job, or for a volunteer position with a local organization, you will have an idea of what the application form will look like. The application will likely ask you to provide the following: a personal statement (an explanation of why you want to participate on the trip), a description of your skills and qualifications, a summary of your prior volunteer and travel experience, an assessment of your language skills (if you are volunteering in a country where English is not the primary language), and your resume or curriculum vitae. If you really want your application to stand out from all the others, spend some time thinking about the special skills and qualifications that you possess, and which will make you an asset to have on the trip. The application process is similar to applying for a job, because this is not the time to be modest about your talents and achievements. Are you multilingual and fluent in many languages? Do you have impressive musical talents? Do your colleagues consider you a cataloging whiz? Are you able to communicate with students in a way that makes you an outstanding teacher? Whatever your unique talents are, be sure to highlight them in your application.

EXPENSES AND FUNDING

Regardless of which type of trip you decide to take, there are a number of pre-trip and in-country expenses for you to consider when planning your trip. Pre-trip costs refer to the items that need to be purchased before you go on your trip, and may include a program fee, airfare, visa, travel insurance, immunizations, and medication. In-country costs refer to all of the expenses that you'll incur once you arrive in your destination country; these include living expenses (accommodation and meals), transportation, and entertainment (travel within the country and/or pre/post-trip travel, Internet cafes, souvenirs, etc.). Your entertainment needs will vary depending on your personal spending habits, but be sure to allow ample room in your budget to explore if you would like to. Figures 4.1, 4.2, and 4.3 show the estimated costs (CAD) for a ten-day volunteer trip in El Salvador.

As you can see, traveling overseas to volunteer isn't cheap. But don't worry; if you're not able to fund your trip yourself, there are a wide variety of fund-raising options available to help you make your dream come true. The popularity of donation-based crowd-funding has grown exponentially in the past few years, and we know quite a few volunteers who were able to fund-raise the entire cost of their trip, or a significant portion (75 percent) of it, through popular websites like Kickstarter, Indiegogo, GoFundMe, Fundrazr, and crowdrise. There are some big benefits to this approach in that you can set up an account quickly and easily share your project page on all of your social media accounts. Project pages with catchy titles, great pictures, and inspiring project descriptions can be extremely successful. The typical fee for using one of these sites is 3 to 5 percent of the money raised via the website.

If you prefer to fund-raise offline, there are countless ways to do it. The most obvious place to begin is with family and friends. If someone close to you refuses to donate at least five dollars to your great cause, you can threaten to post an embarrassing picture of them on Facebook. If they're still hesitant, tell them that you'll also post the picture on Instagram and then tweet it to your 10,000+ followers. We promise you that this strategy is really effective! At work, you can always drop in on your colleagues in their offices, tell them about your project, and ask them to donate. You may be surprised just how eager people will be to help. Before one of my trips, I asked my col-

FIGURE 4.1
Sample organized service trip, El Salvador (ten days)

ITEM	COST
Passport	$160.00
Program Fee	$1600.00
Airfare + Transportation	$600.00
Visa	N/A
Travel Insurance	$100.00
Immunizations	$300.00
Prescription Medication	$50.00
Miscellaneous	$200.00
TOTAL	$3010.00

FIGURE 4.2
Sample DIY trip, El Salvador (ten days)

ITEM	COST
Passport	$160.00
Airfare + Transportation	$600.00
Visa	N/A
Travel Insurance	$60.00
Immunizations	$300.00
Accommodation (apartment)	$600 and up
Food	$150 and up
Medication	$50.00
Miscellaneous	$200.00
TOTAL	$2120.00

leagues (face to face) for donations for collection development, and I raised a little over $200 in an hour. That's a large amount of money for such a small effort. Another tried-and-true method is to hold some type of special event. The last bake sale I helped organize raised over $300. You read that right! We made more than $300 selling homemade cookies and brownies.

TAKING TIME OFF FROM WORK

We know that some of you are thinking that you would love to volunteer and have a lot to offer, but how can you get away from work for a week (or two, or more)? The easiest way to manage this is to use your personal vacation time. Most of us receive three or four weeks of vacation each year, so if you don't have any other options, you could use this one. There are other types

FIGURE 4.3

Sample structured trip, El Salvador (ten days)

ITEM	COST
Passport	$160.00
Program Fee	$500.00
Airfare + Transportation	$600.00
Visa	N/A
Travel Insurance	$60.00
Immunizations	$300.00
Medication	$50.00
Miscellaneous*	$200.00
TOTAL	$1870.00

Accommodation and meals provided via homestay with a local family.

*Miscellaneous items include: buses, taxis, meals in restaurants, entertainment, trips to tourist attractions, souvenirs, etc.

of leave alternatives available to academic librarians. For instance, you may be entitled to a certain number of research or professional development days each year. If you have a research interest in international librarianship, you could consider writing an article or giving a conference presentation based on your experience. Another great option available to academic librarians is to volunteer while on sabbatical. We've met quite a few public librarian volunteers whose employers simply gave them the time off to participate in a service trip. The volunteers made the case that the experience would inform their practice by enhancing their teaching, leadership, or teamwork skills, and as a result, they didn't have to use their vacation or professional development days to volunteer abroad. Of course, your ability to make a successful argument depends in part on your job title, professional responsibilities, and the demographics of the local community that your library serves.

PRE-TRIP PREPARATION: ASK THE RIGHT QUESTIONS

It is important for you to have a clear understanding of the project work that you'll be participating in before you depart for your trip. Most organized and structured trips will provide you with complete background information about the project; review the project's goals and your role in helping to achieve those goals. The organization will also provide any necessary training, either before you leave on your trip, once you arrive at your destination, or in both locations. If it isn't covered in an information session or training, one essential question to ask is how the organization will measure the trip's success. The answer will allow you to determine if their goals align with your goals and will help you know what to expect. If you plan a DIY trip, be sure to carefully consider the project's objectives and training opportunities before you agree to volunteer.

You know how employers love to include the "performs other duties as assigned" clause in job descriptions? This clause allows them to ask you to do anything that is not considered a regular part of your job. As an international volunteer, it is crucial to ask whether you might be assigned work that is outside the scope of what you signed up for. For example, if you agreed to lead children's literacy classes for elementary school students in Belize, is it possible that you would be asked to provide instruction for secondary students? Or will you be asked to assist in the construction of a new elementary school? Or will you be requested to document the trip by writing 1,000 words a day and posting daily project updates to the organization's website?

Regardless of where you are volunteering, ask if there is a dress code to which you need to adhere. Some countries, or regions within a country (which you might not expect), have strict cultural expectations about what is deemed appropriate for people (especially women) to wear in public. Before we traveled to Chajul in Guatemala, we were informed that women are expected to wear skirts and shorts that are at least knee-length, and loose-fitting, crew neck–style shirts. Another thing for you to inquire about is whether your group will have a designated interpreter. As you can imagine, having someone who is responsible for ensuring that your group understands what is going on, what is being asked of them in any situation, or even just to read the daily special on a menu is extremely helpful.

PRE-TRIP PREPARATION: PACK THE RIGHT ATTITUDE

Regardless of the type of trip you go on, you'll need to pack your soft skills. These should include nearly endless quantities of adaptability, flexibility, patience, and open-mindedness. The need for adaptability may come up when you least expect it. Imagine that 99 percent of your trip has exceeded your expectations: all of your flights (and baggage) arrived on time, your projects were interesting and challenging, and you feel like you made a valuable difference. Your group has a visit to a major tourist destination planned and is ready to depart when the trip is suddenly canceled due to an impromptu street protest. As unlikely as this may sound, it could happen. Your reaction to a scenario like this will affect not only your mood, but the emotions of all the other group members as well. It would be a complete waste of time, energy, and work if you allowed a single incident like this to ruin your day, your week, or the overall trip experience.

Since international volunteering can be extremely difficult for even the most flexible of people, we don't recommend it to people who like to make and stick to precise plans and those who aren't fans of compromise. Situa-

Consider a Cold Call

THOUGH I ONLY make and receive them occasionally, I've always been fascinated by the potential power of cold calls (and cold e-mails) to establish new professional connections, be they one-offs, weak links, or more reciprocal, enduring relationships. Some organizations publish the names of past volunteer trip participants on their website, so you're able to look them up and contact them. Don't be afraid to reach out to them; they may be able to provide valuable insights that help you decide if a certain trip is likely to provide you with the experiences you're looking for. I've had people contact me with a list of questions, and I enjoyed the opportunity for reminiscing that arose as I took the time to provide them with thorough responses.

Dee Winn, Quebec, Canada

tions that require flexibility will constantly pop up, and you need to be not only open to, but also willing to accept changes as they come. On one trip I made to Guatemala, I was a member of the Cataloging Team and our major goal was to catalog all of the new books. We were lucky enough to have one bilingual Spanish speaker on our team . . . until he wasn't on it. It turned out that the Programming Team needed his language skills even more than we did. How much time did we spend whining about how unfair this was? Did we spend our time complaining that he was a member of our team, not their team, and grumbling that since none of us knew Spanish, our task had just gotten a lot harder? Not for a minute, not even a single second! We were all flexible, and we realized that we were there as a team of thirteen volunteers, all working together to achieve a major goal. Keeping that in mind allowed us to carry on with our work as though nothing at all had changed.

It is impossible to overstate the importance of having an abundance of patience when you volunteer overseas. There is a Swahili proverb that says, "Patience attracts happiness; it brings near that which is far." This quote is a priceless piece of wisdom to remember when you've been cataloging books for four hours, and then a school librarian asks you to stop using the agreed-upon classification system and redo all of your work using a different classification system. Those words would also serve you well if you've spent an entire morning lifting and carrying heavy cinder blocks to create the foundation for a school library, and then the project coordinator tells you that the blocks have been placed in the wrong spot. These scenarios weren't made up; they actually happened . . . to us! We promise you that you'll need patience on any international volunteer trip you participate in.

By open-mindedness, we mean that you need to fully embrace the opportunity to have new experiences, be put in new situations, and be exposed to new ideas and ways of doing things. Showers with freezing cold water? No big deal. Meals that are not gluten-free or low-carb? That is definitely going to happen. Stomach bugs like nothing you've ever experienced before? Be prepared, and pack Cipro! Unidentified insects in your bed? Yikes! Having unanticipated time when you just sit around, and don't feel like you're contributing? These instances should be rare, but they can happen. Are you feeling lonely, or homesick, or are you craving a Big Mac? Don't worry; most people feel that way at some point in the trip. Trust us, these feelings will pass. As the popular education quote states: "Don't be afraid to be open-minded. Your brain isn't going to fall out." Wherever you decide to volunteer, you will constantly be exposed to new situations, new experiences, and new people. At some point during the trip, you may have to revise your original expectations, or be willing and able to accept that you're in a difficult situation or are required to work with a difficult person. Being adaptable, flexible, patient, and open-minded (even if these traits don't come naturally to you) will help to ensure a successful trip. One final attribute that must be mentioned is common sense. Some countries that you visit may not be as safe as the country you live in. The Canadian government has published a travel guide titled *Her Own Way: A Woman's Safe-Travel Guide* (https://travel.gc .ca/travelling/publications/her-own-way), and the U.S. State Department has a "Traveler's Checklist" that provides health and safety tips for traveling abroad (https://travel.state.gov/content/passports/en/go.html). We recommend that you take a look at one (or both) of these resources before your trip.

Since English is my first and only language, I took a Spanish class to prepare for my first international volunteer trip to a country with an official language other than English. I admit, I thought this was a genius move that would allow me to become as bilingual as I needed to be for my eleven-day adventure. I'd like to tell you that it was one of the best things I did to prepare for the trip, but I'd be lying. Essentially, I spent a lot of time and money to learn that "ll" is pronounced like a "y," "hello" is hola, and "thank you" is gracias. To be honest, I already knew these things (and that cerveza means "beer"), so the sole benefit from the sixteen weeks of class was mastering the phrases "My name is Dee" and "I'm from Canada!" in Spanish.

PRE-TRIP PREPARATION: PACK THE RIGHT STUFF

Once you've mentally prepared for the trip, you can get down to the nitty-gritty of deciding what to bring. A few of the things you need to bring are so obvious we almost didn't include them in this section, but for the record, these items include your passport (plus a photocopy in case you lose the original), plane ticket (or e-ticket), travel visa (if required), vaccination certification (Carte Jaune/Yellow Card, if required), an itinerary of your trip, and local currency (if possible). Clearly, you also need to bring clothing that is appropriate for the climate and the work that you'll be doing (don't forget to ask about a dress code). Even if you are traveling to a place that is usually much warmer than where you live, be sure to pack a few warm clothes, just in case the temperature is much lower than you (and weather forecasters) anticipated. Like so many things in this book, this tip allows you to learn from our mistakes. To my complete shock, Honolulu was unseasonably cold in January, while I was there to attend the Hawai'i International Conference on Education. I did not have appropriate clothing, and to my regret, I had left my parka at home.

If you only follow one piece of advice in this entire book, we hope it is this: pack as much hand sanitizer as you can. Go to the dollar store and buy every bottle (under 100 mls) that they have on the shelves. If they only have five bottles, go back tomorrow and buy more. We realize that hand sanitizers may kill good bacteria and dry out your hands to the point that moisturizer will then become your most-prized possession, but trust us on this one! You will find yourself in many situations every single day that call for generous amounts of hand sanitizer. Actually, we have another piece of advice that you must follow. Be sure to book an appointment with a doctor at a travel clinic once you've confirmed your trip. Depending on your destination, they are likely to provide you with a prescription for Ciprofloxacin (Cipro), and we beg you to fill that prescription. Cipro is used to treat the unpleasant condition known as traveler's diarrhea. You can acquire this illness by ingesting contaminated food or water. The symptoms are not limited to diarrhea and also include nausea, abdominal cramping, vomiting, fever, painful gas, and bloating. According to the Canadian government's travel information website, traveler's diarrhea is "the most common illness that affects travelers," and the high-risk areas are "developing countries in Central and South America, Mexico, Africa, the Middle East, and Asia." Trust us, you or one of your fellow travelers will be very glad that you brought Cipro! Other random items that you may want to bring include toilet paper, a flashlight, a diary, a reusable water bottle, wet wipes, a first aid kit, pictures of your loved ones, books, earplugs, and a camera or smartphone.

We hope that you have learned a lot from reading this chapter, and if you still feel a bit unprepared, know this—you're a lot more prepared than we were, because this book didn't exist when we began volunteering internationally! Your trip will be similar to your gym membership; you will get out of it exactly what you put into it. If you select the type of trip that best fits your qualifications and personality, have a firm understanding of the work that will be expected of you, prepare as much as you can, and maintain a positive attitude no matter what comes your way, then you are sure to have a memorable experience.

chapter 5

If Only I Had Known
Dos, Don'ts, and Practical Advice

I CLEARLY RECALL THE FIRST NIGHT OF MY VERY FIRST VOLUNTEER trip to Central America. I was in a hostel, perched on the bottom of a kids' size bunk bed in a hot damp room with at least eight other female librarians and LIS students from around the world. All of us were complete strangers, some young, some older, some quietly processing the new locale, others very loud and excited and bursting at the seams to get started; I fell firmly into the older, quieter category. When my head hit the hard, small pillow I was overcome with homesickness, missing my family and the comforts of home, and very jealous of the second- and third-timers who knew to bring their own pillows and sleep aids. I started a list that night of "things I should have brought" in case I survived the week and chose to ever volunteer again. I'm happy to say I survived, thrived, and lived to volunteer again, and the moral of my sad tale is: *be prepared!* In the words of Benjamin Franklin, "By failing to prepare, you are preparing to fail," or as Alexander Graham Bell liked to say, "Before anything else, preparation is the key to success." I think it is safe to say that these two gentlemen have given advice that should be heeded. While the Boy Scouts know all about being prepared, this librarian quickly learned the peril of not being prepared. But preparation is just one aspect of a successful international volunteer trip. There are many dos and don'ts that international volunteers have learned through experience and which will be of benefit to others, both newbies and seasoned pros alike.

Dos and Don'ts

Dealing with fickle Mother Nature, transporting supplies, staying healthy; there is lots to think about before getting on that plane.

MOTHER NATURE

I experienced my first earthquake while in Central America on my first volunteer trip, and I was unaware of what was happening. I chalk this up to my limited worldview at the time. When our group was discussing the quake later in the day, this greatly affected one younger volunteer who became quite anxious about earthquakes. I chose to view the event as a unique occurrence that not many experience and that I would not have experienced back home. Since that trip, I have witnessed one other minor earthquake while visiting libraries in Mexico, and I'm proud to say I recognized the event the second

Let It Go

WHEN VOLUNTEERING INTERNATIONALLY, don't hold on to home too tightly. The opportunity to travel is the opportunity to immerse yourself in a totally new culture. If you don't make new friends, and go to local bars and restaurants and eat local food, you're missing out on the most rewarding parts of international volunteerism. Many places will offer the familiarity of home (McDonald's exists everywhere!), so it takes a conscious effort to break out of your comfort zone and throw yourself head-first into your adventure. You should also be prepared for and accommodating of unexpected delays. Other parts of the world may operate on a different schedule than you are used to, so look out for opportunities to explore. While interning in Africa, my book shipment was delayed for months in transit, so I took a two-month overland trip across the continent, and it was the most rewarding experience of my life!

Christina Wilson, New York, U.S.A.

time when I awoke to feel my bed shaking at 2:00 a.m. While volunteering in Nicaragua in the rainy season, I was exposed to daily sudden downpours and the inconvenience of mud-clogged roads and pathways. The trip to Nicaragua was to an area where an entire town had been relocated after their homes, churches, and schools had been destroyed in a mudslide three years earlier. Experiencing the rain and knee-deep mud at firsthand reinforced for me why that remote community, located at the base of a volcano, needed volunteers and assistance. My brief exposure to the minor inconvenience of rain and mud was also an important reminder that the community had experienced catastrophic, life-changing conditions that I would probably never have to experience myself. This was another opportunity to count my blessings and recommit myself to helping those who are in need. The rainy season in Honduras also reminded me of the wrath of Mother Nature and its effect on life in certain areas of the world. I chose to volunteer a few weeks after the rainy season was supposed to end, but was told on arrival that the rainy season was delayed about a month that year. The constant heavy downpours washed out the water lines (hollow bamboo and cut-up bits of rubber hose) that ran through the trees to the apartment I had rented. The caretaker would reinstall these pipes daily and they would then wash away again, leaving the toilet and sink inoperable. This proved challenging and stressful for the first few days, but I forced myself to stay calm and make an effort to adopt the local attitude that it would eventually be fixed, and my frustration and stress were of no use. Earthquakes, hurricanes, mudslides, and other natural disasters are often the reason why international volunteers are needed to assist in affected libraries in the first place, but they can also occur while volunteers are on the ground. It is wise to research the weather for the time you will be traveling and to look into the likelihood of any extreme occurrences during your trip. Traveling outside of rainy seasons whenever possible is also advisable!

STREET FOOD

In certain regions and countries, it is wise to avoid eating street food. While the corn on the cob for sale from a barbecue on a street corner may look delicious, and you have never tried the colorful fruits being offered from a basket perched on a street vendor's head, in regions where it is unsafe to drink the water, it is advisable to forgo eating anything that is not commercially prepared. Having seen the ensuing illness when colleagues have dared to purchase such delicacies in Central America, I can't stress this enough. Some street vendors may wash their offerings with the local tap water, if they wash them at all, and the vendors may not be regulated by any governing body with regard to hygiene, storage, and preparation. An image of a street vendor in Guatemala who walked away from his barbecue stand to relieve himself on the side of the road and then promptly returned to selling his wares is forever burned in my memory. Err on the side of caution and stick to commercial restaurants, prepackaged food, and items you prepare yourself. This doesn't mean you can't try those unique local fruits; just purchase them at the grocery store and wash and cut them yourself (see figure 5.1).

FIGURE 5.1
Boil It, Peel It:
Street food graphic

Boil it...
peel it...
cook it...
wash it...
or forget it!

LIBRARY SUPPLIES

Transporting supplies for libraries in need can be somewhat problematic. Very remote libraries and schools may not be accessible by vehicle and may not have a postal address for deliveries. A community school I visited in Ometepe required a one-hour drive and then a one-hour hike through the muddy jungle on foot. The island of Roatan in Honduras is also very difficult to ship supplies to and required that I deliver them in person. It is beneficial to liaise with the library staff prior to travel and solicit a "wish list" of supplies needed. In my experience, these lists often involve office supplies such as tape, glue, labeling stickers, and staplers, and school and program supplies such as paper, crayons, and markers. Requests for specific books or genres in both English and the native languages are also common. One wish list I received included kitchen timers to be used during homework help sessions, chess sets, puppets, and household cleaning products for science lessons. Transporting supplies in an old throw-away suitcase is advisable since it is relatively inexpensive to pay for one extra case (approximately $25), and you can leave the suitcase behind when you return home. Books are heavy and therefore can be ordered online and the shipping designated directly to the host library from the online bookstore. Using third-party shipping companies can be costly and is not recommended unless all other options have been ruled out. The Oaxaca Lending Library (OLL) in Mexico has created a reference resource list or "wish list" on its website listing titles that the library needs for its collection. Volunteers, visitors, or tourists are urged to bring one or two of the books on the list with them when they visit Oaxaca. Donors and volunteers can also request that an OLL staffer purchase and ship the books to the volunteer or visitor in the United States, and then that person will bring the titles with them when they travel. This is another example of the importance of not relying on third-party shipping in some areas of the world.

One *Vitumbua*, Two *Vitumbua* . . .

MOST PEOPLE WILL tell you how long they spent overseas. I count my time in Tanzania by the number of *vitumbua* I ate. The little golden fried rice cakes are heavenly, especially when sprinkled with a little powdered sugar. I developed a truly loving relationship with these African donuts, and I encourage any international librarian to discover her own food love affair. By the time I left, the little old lady who sold them knew exactly how many I would buy (too many) and would always smile and throw one in for free. My Swahili was worse than her English, but we had a deep understanding. I still dream of them to this day, but have to satisfy myself with making chipsi mayai, the egg-covered fries served as common street food, at home instead.

Christina Wilson, New York, U.S.A.

When faced with large wish lists, I sometimes seek donations from my colleagues and friends. Oftentimes people in my networks have extra supplies they are happy to donate, or funds to help purchase or ship items. Colleagues have donated school supplies their children did not use, and library supplies no longer needed such as card pockets and labeling stickers. One year I solicited donations for supplies through an online crowd-sourcing site, and I used the donations to purchase books to be shipped directly. I then made stickers with the name of each person who donated, and I attached these "Donated by _____ from _____ (country name)" stickers to the front of the books. Another year, a department at the university where I work donated funds to purchase books and cover the shipping. I have also received donations in the name of a deceased loved one and their commitment to literacy, and I embossed the donated books with their name; that name is now living on and proudly displayed in books in libraries in Central America.

On a recent service trip to Central America, the trip leader told me about a rule he follows when donating supplies on his trips. The leader does not give the supplies directly to the children in need; instead, he arranges to hand over the supplies behind closed doors to the library staff or to the teachers who requested the materials. The local staff can then decide how to allocate the various supplies if they are giving some to local schoolchildren and patrons, and they hand them out when and how they wish. The leader feels it is important that the volunteers or outsiders are not seen as swooping in and saving the day, but that the supplies come from the authorities of the local institution. This avoids any negative perception of reliance on outside agencies and also allows the local staff to decide how to use the supplies. This private exchange of items also eliminates any awkwardness on the part of the host agency, or feelings of indebtedness or the need for conspicuous displays of gratitude. Having purchased and delivered large boxes of crayons for a recent service-learning trip, I noted that the schoolteacher receiving the supplies chose to separate the large boxes of crayons into their smaller internal boxes and hand those smaller boxes out to the local children, thereby making the supplies go further. Had I handed the supplies directly to the children, or done so in front of them, this clever "stretching of supplies" would not have occurred. The staff know what they need and why, so trust them and don't assume that you know best.

PERSONAL SUPPLIES

It is also a good idea to bring some unique personal supplies for yourself, any families you may stay with, and your colleagues at the host library. When I volunteer, I always travel with tea bags, raisins, vitamins, red licorice, chocolate, an extra travel blanket, and pleasure-reading materials. These are items I rely on at home, and they help me if I am feeling homesick or overwhelmed while traveling. They are also items that are more difficult to purchase in some of the areas where I volunteer. In addition, I bring distinctly Canadian items (maple syrup, maple sugar, Canada-themed lanyards, office or library-related items with my institution's logo, etc.) in case I wish to give a small gift to colleagues or homestay families. Stickers, coloring pencils and crayons, and small toys are always a big hit with homestay children and the children of colleagues, and these items take up little room in a suitcase.

CULTURE SHOCK

While bringing favorite personal items from home will help with culture shock, the latter is a condition that is hard to avoid. The *Merriam-Webster Dictionary* defines culture shock as "a sense of confusion and uncertainty, sometimes with feelings of anxiety, that may affect people exposed to an alien culture or environment without adequate preparation,"[1] and such feelings are commonly part of the international volunteer experience. While not everyone will go through the stages of culture shock in order, or even experience all the stages, there are four well-known stages: honeymoon, crisis, recovery, and adjustment (see figure 5.2).[2] With experience, I have come to learn that my feelings of culture shock in the "crisis" phase are most intense during my first two days volunteering in a new country, particularly during my first night away. And I know that once I reach day three I start to "recover"; that is, I no longer feel anxious or alone, and am more comfortable with my new surroundings and eager to soak up new experiences. In speaking with other volunteers, I have learned that the majority go through this same initial bout of culture shock, though some never feel any anxiety or unease. But, I have also traveled with a couple of volunteers who suffered extreme anxiety from the moment they set foot in the airport to the moment they returned home. While international volunteering was not for them, and I doubt they would choose to travel again, most volunteers succumb to an initial minor period of culture shock which they quickly overcome as they forge new relationships and get involved in the actual volunteer work.

Keeping busy, being open to new experiences and new relationships, recognizing and appreciating the unfamiliar, and bringing personal comfort items from home will help you make the initial transition. Recognizing your own anxiety and talking openly and sharing your feelings with co-volunteers and trip leaders are also beneficial (see figure 5.3). As someone

FIGURE 5.2
Culture shock

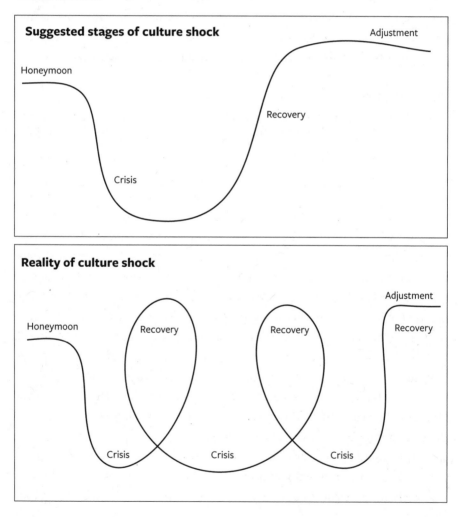

who suffered from extreme homesickness as a child, and who could not sleep away from home until much later in life, I take pride in recognizing and then being able to overcome my feelings of anxiety on arriving in new countries.

FIGURE 5.3
When faced with culture shock

DO	DON'T
✓ Stay busy	✗ Make big decisions or overreact
✓ Acknowledge and share your feelings with fellow travelers and trip leaders (no shame!)	✗ Seclude yourself
	✗ Fixate on the differences, instead acknowledge and celebrate them
✓ Notice the familiar but also appreciate the unfamiliar	✗ Mistake different for wrong
✓ Seek out and discuss shared interests with colleagues and travelers (similarities in the culture, the workplace, similar family structure, mutual hobbies)	✗ Cause initial unnecessary worry for family and friends back home with constant complaints; give yourself time to adjust
✓ Purchase familiar food and drink until you are comfortable trying new delicacies	✗ Criticize or judge your host country, customs and/or colleagues
✓ Keep a journal (to express your feelings and also to recognize and overcome such feelings on future trips)	✗ Feel shamed or a sense of failure, culture shock is natural and different for everyone
✓ Find a friend or advisor to help with local customs and language	✗ Neglect your personal routines (diet, exercise, sleep) so drastically that your health suffers
✓ Set goals	✗ Insist on communicating in your own language; instead make an effort to learn key phrases in the local language and become more independent
✓ Celebrate small victories	
✓ Get plenty of rest	

COMMUNICATION

Maintaining communication with family and colleagues back home while volunteering internationally can be challenging, but it is not impossible. The prevalence of cell phones and Wi-Fi has made communication much easier. I am continually surprised by the access to Wi-Fi in remote areas, and I have seen this access increase yearly in my travels. The prevalence of personal cell phones among locals who may not even be able to afford the basics of life always surprises me. Gone are the days of calling cards and pay phones, posting letters, and relaying messages. Volunteers may choose to purchase inexpensive "throwaway" cell phones for volunteer trips, phones that will not be missed if lost or stolen. Depending on where one is volunteering, it might be cumbersome and impractical to travel with a laptop or tablet and wiser to instead utilize the computers at the host organization, school, or library. Check ahead to see if such access is available. If traveling in an organized group, group leaders will invariably have a cell phone for emergencies that can be used when necessary. While traveling in Guatemala, our group of volunteers regularly spent evenings at a local Internet cafe that offered both Wi-Fi and North American coffee and tea. This ritual allowed volunteers to communicate daily with family and friends and also to catch up on any school or work assignments requiring their attention; it was also good bonding time for a group of strangers traveling together.

SOCIAL MEDIA

According to the Pew Research Center, seven out of ten Americans currently use social media, with Facebook, Twitter, Pinterest, Instagram, and LinkedIn being the preferred platforms.[3] LIS professionals use social media to connect and engage with their customers and their employees, as well as their family and friends. Social media are also an integral part of volunteering in libraries internationally. If you are comfortable doing so, social media can be a good tool for fund-raising prior to a trip. Spread the word in your online networks that you are volunteering and could use donations of supplies, or funds to purchase supplies and books. Crowd-funding platforms such as Go Fund Me, Fundrazr, and Causevox (to name a few) can also be leveraged, but keep in mind that some platforms charge a fee or take a percentage of monetary donations.

Prior to travel, social media can also be beneficial for connecting with the host library and staff:

- Follow the host library's pages and become informed on the programs and services the library offers.
- Reach out and "friend" staff so that you have made a connection and can communicate prior to arrival.

- Generate excitement about your trip if you are traveling with a group that likes to use social media to recruit new donors and participants.

Once on the ground in your new location, you can also use social media to communicate with friends and family back home, to share pictures and news, and to pay it forward by describing the needs of your host library (or community) and possibly generating interest in future volunteer or fund-raising opportunities. Communicating via e-mail can be problematic with differing time zones, as can writing out a long e-mail and then waiting a day for the recipient to read and have the time to respond. It is much easier to simply post or message a photo or quick note and check in when time allows. While there was not always time for me to send long e-mails to my family, I was able to post a picture now and then so they knew where I was and could follow my journeys. Some service trips offered by nonprofit groups encourage volunteers to use their social media pages to educate others about the need for volunteers and to generate interest in future trips. Frequently, such trips will recruit volunteers who are interested in or very experienced with marketing and social media to create content for their pages while traveling. If this is a particular interest, ask group leaders if they would like you to create a social media team or will let you be responsible for those pages while volunteering. It always bears repeating that you must remember to follow the same rules of social media as you would in your own library when it comes to photos and permissions, professional conduct, and so on. Err on the side of caution and be cognizant of the fact that you will be representing not only the host library, but the nonprofit you may be traveling with (and your co-volunteers on the trip who will share your posts), your own employer back home, and even Great Aunt Sally who is proudly following and sharing your every adventure. We have all seen the pictures on Facebook of a parent with a sign that reads, "Please share this post so I can show my kids how far and how fast posts travel"; posts travel very far and very fast, and they stick with you for a long time. Strive to be politically correct, culturally sensitive, positive, and informative. Finally, once your trip is complete and you are back at your regular job, social media are a quick and easy way to keep abreast of goings-on at the library you visited, share their news, programs, and activities, and keep in touch with staff and new friends. After returning home from Honduras, I was thrilled to notice on the host library's Facebook page that one of my program ideas for increasing pleasure reading at their library was being successfully implemented; this was a rewarding surprise.

FOLLOW-UP

It is very important to keep in touch with your host library and staff after your visit. You should try to make sure that your relationship with your host library is not just a one-time charitable visit but, as Librarians Without Borders founder Melanie Sellars states, "is reciprocal, action-oriented, and focused on advancing our shared profession." Sellars suggests that international librarians "move our activities beyond short-term charity work or descriptive studies into work that can have an influential and long-lasting impact."[4] Since volunteering in Honduras, I have kept in touch with the library's founder and the librarian. While they have sent charitable funding requests, they have also requested lesson-planning materials for the teachers they visit on their bookmobiles, as well as links to literacy materials and resources. We have discussed future trips and areas requiring attention, and we have shared our successes and ideas. The university where I work has an ongoing relationship with the governing organization, as well as with a professor who conducts teacher training through that library. This ongoing reciprocal relationship will be very helpful if and when I am planning to return. Follow-up can take many forms, from something as simple as checking up via social media, to e-mails, phone calls, or the sharing of links, articles, and resources. I once toured a community library in Nicaragua that was created by an American expatriate, and this library has a unique system for ongoing voluntary cataloging of its collection. A retired American cataloger who had volunteered with the library is now its full-time cataloger-at-a-distance. The expatriate library founder in Nicaragua takes new items to be cataloged to her home state when she visits, where the cataloger also lives, and the volunteer catalogs the material in her home with the applicable software. The library founder then transports the cataloged materials back to the library when she returns to Nicaragua. This is an ongoing partnership and a mutually beneficial arrangement between a cataloger who is not yet ready to step away from her passion and a library in need of volunteer services.

MINDSET

As with dessert, I have saved the best till last. The most important advice I can offer is that you should maintain an open mind and be flexible! I guarantee you that with international volunteer work, nothing will go as planned. Flights will be canceled and delayed; you will arrive to find schools and libraries you were supposed to work in unexpectedly closed; facilities, software, and collections will not be as they were represented; staff you had liaised with for months may suddenly no longer be available; you may become ill and unable to complete what you had hoped; things may be "lost in translation"; the accommodations may not be what you had been promised; and supplies may arrive late or not at all. At the risk of scaring off future volunteers, I must highlight the importance of remaining open-minded, calm, and able to cope with unexpected occurrences. Remember back in chapter 2 when I wrote that volunteer work reduces stress and blood pressure and improves mood? Well, those health benefits are only possible if you keep a level head and roll with the punches when things don't go as planned.

- A+ for Flexibility
- Acclimate yourself.
- Accommodate unexpected occurrences and differences.
- Adapt.
- Alter course when necessary.
- Accept the situation and make the best of it.

I have volunteered in many countries where time is relative, schedules and appointments are very loose and are viewed as mere suggestions, and there is a belief that things will get done when they get done and nothing happens in a hurry. I have learned to adapt and leave my Canadian agenda and my clock worshipping back home when I volunteer internationally. Don't become anxious or stressed and unable to continue your work when you find a gecko crawling out of a library book and up your arm. Do as I did when this happened; scream silently in your head, shake the poor creature off of your arm, resolve to be a bit more observant, and get back to work. What do you do if you are on a group volunteer trip and you find yourself rooming with someone who is your complete opposite in every way, there is no room to

Grandmothers Know Best

MY GRANDMOTHER'S SAGE advice has helped me in my international life. She said that when I am out to dinner in public, I should:

1. Never discuss politics.
I lived in Oman the year after the 9/11 attacks. With helicopters shaking the school as they flew over on missions to Iraq, anti-American feeling reached an all-time high. While not expressed openly, it crept out in the form of jokes in meetings and the teachers' lounge.

The school's head was Canadian, but of foreign descent, and turned a blind eye to the situation. As a seasoned expatriate, I had a tough hide and a sense of humor, but it was disheartening to be heckled. (The difference between the United States and yogurt? If you leave yogurt alone for 300 years, it develops a culture.)

One day, however, at the beginning of a tedious staff meeting, a Canadian teacher stood up and quietly said, "As an international school, isn't our mission to accept and treat all equally? We need, then, to stop picking on Americans." Mouths fell open in shock, mine included. Murmuring assent followed, with many people studying their shoes. I can't say his comment solved the problem, but his brave, kind gesture helped make people aware of the power of unkind words.

2. Never discuss religion.
While working in Saudi Arabia I had two volunteers; one Indian and a Hindu, the other Pakistani and Muslim. My principal stressed the importance of separating them, so I posted the ALA Code of Ethics, and followed her advice.

This separate but equal policy continued until the day the circulation computer died in the middle of two class visits. With kids swarming everywhere and only fifteen minutes to check out more than 100 books, I called for all hands on deck, forgetting in the panic the "keep-apart" mandate. We all pitched in and when the job was done, I made coffee for us all: American, Indian, Canadian, Brazilian, Pakistani, Jamaican; and Muslim, Christian, Hindu.

We drank it while sharing stories, laughing at the zaniness of the day. After which, we all got back to work; but with a change. From then on we worked where we needed and wanted to, and I didn't worry about separating people. Religion, because it was not the focus, did not divide us.

3. Never order chicken on the bone.
It is inelegant and makes a mess.

Sarah Gibson, Florida, U.S.A.

switch, and it is obvious you will never have any kind of connection with her? After making an effort to connect on some level (you both love libraries don't you?), take the opportunity to learn from the experience, spend more time working and seeing the local attractions instead of staying in the room, and feel grateful for how wonderful your living arrangements and friends are on your return home. Does the Wi-Fi or the electricity go down while you are working on a project in the host library? Be creative, go back to those old skills with paper and pen, conduct an impromptu read-aloud, story time, or craft program, or come up with a plan that the staff can use in future when power outages occur. The ability to adapt and improvise, to be creative and flexible, will serve you well while volunteering, but also when you return to your regular life..

Now You Know

While every volunteer expedition is different, as is every volunteer, the dos and don'ts espoused here all come from personal experience. Being prepared for every eventuality is impossible, but these dos and don'ts should serve to help new volunteers avoid some of the pitfalls that others have been faced with. Mother Nature will always surprise you, but planning your trip for the optimal time in that foreign country will go a long way to ensuring a safer and more positive experience. Being aware of the possible pitfalls that can arise with communication, the transporting of supplies, and the purchasing of food is just common sense. Those who never experience culture shock are lucky individuals, but for those who do experience it, recognition of the stages involved and how best to navigate them is very important to well-being. And despite all of these possible pitfalls, and accompanying warnings and directives, volunteering feels good and is good for you! Remaining flexible, putting aside those rigid routines and notions, and improvising and adjusting when necessary will ensure that you can cash in on that lowered blood pressure and improvement in mood. Let's do it together: deep breath, relax, regroup, it'll all get done.

Notes

1. *Merriam-Webster Dictionary*, 2017, https://www.merriam-webster.com/dictionary/culture%20shock.

2. Rachel Irwin, "Culture Shock: Negotiating Feelings in the Field," *Anthropology Matters* 9 (2007), https://www.anthropologymatters.com/index.php/anth_matters/article/view/64/123.

3. "Social Media Fact Sheet," Pew Research Center, 2017, www.pewinternet.org/fact-sheet/social-media.

4. Melanie Sellars, "Strategies for Engaging in International Librarianship: Misconceptions and Opportunities," San Jose State University, 2016, http://scholarworks.sjsu.edu/slissrj/vol6/iss1/2.

chapter 6

Home Again, Home Again... Now What?

Reentry

So your trip is complete and you've returned home full of energy and renewed commitment, with plans for the future, stories to tell, and knowledge and pictures to share. Now what? While your return to regular life may cause some discomfort, and reverse culture shock may occur, now is the time to harness that energy, transfer your knowledge, solidify partnerships, share your experiences, and advocate!

REVERSE CULTURE SHOCK

Most travelers are aware of culture shock and the accompanying feelings of anxiety when they are suddenly immersed in a new culture and way of life. As a frequent traveler, I was well aware of the possibility of culture shock prior to my first international volunteer experience, and I recognized the signs and stages when they occurred. What I wasn't aware of, or prepared for, was reverse culture shock on my return home. I had not heard of the term, I didn't know reverse culture shock existed, and I didn't expect the thoughts and feelings I was having. Well, I quickly learned that reverse culture shock is a reality. The U.S. State Department describes reverse culture shock as "the psychological, emotional and cultural aspects of re-entry." The department's website, which is intended for U.S. military and foreign service workers but is useful for anyone working overseas, touches on change and the fact that "home has changed. You have changed. You have adapted to another culture and now you must readapt."[1]

On arrival back home, international volunteers may experience common symptoms of reverse culture shock, including:

- A newfound awareness of the waste and excess of typical North American culture (feelings of *too much* and *too many* after living in a culture of *not enough*)
- Anxiety about returning to the North American pace of life and values after a slower or different pace of life while away
- A disconnect with colleagues, friends, and family who did not share your experiences
- Missing the new culture and people, and returning to the same unchanging day-to-day life despite feeling that you have changed
- Missing the autonomy, responsibility, and empowerment of traveling and working on your own

As Craig Storti notes in his book *The Art of Coming Home*, the effects of reverse culture shock can include feeling marginalized, critical, overwhelmed, exhausted, and possibly experiencing self-doubt, withdrawal, and depression.[2] As with culture shock, reverse culture shock may vary from person to person, and the depth and intensity of the experience will be affected by many factors: the individual's previous travel experience; her length of time away; the degree of difference between the home environment and the foreign locale; available supports; comfort level with change; and the depth of immersion in the foreign culture while away.

So, how do you deal with reverse culture shock after having volunteered internationally? Some important work can be done before leaving your host country, as well as upon your return home:

- Say goodbye to your new friends and colleagues and ensure that you have their contact information.
- Make concrete plans for ongoing support and communication, a virtual meet-up in the future, or future volunteer trip(s).

- Collect items and souvenirs to share back home, and as reminders of your time away.
- Share your professional development, practices, and experiences with colleagues and friends on your return (see the next tip).
- Know who to share with and when enough is enough; not everyone will want to hear of your travels and see your photos.
- Become involved in activities and groups that relate to your experience (perhaps a newfound love of yoga, new culinary practices, or

Guatemala: There and Back

MY FIRST INTERNATIONAL volunteer experience was to Guatemala, and I experienced culture shock at both ends, going and coming back. I will always remember walking down a long, narrow airport corridor to the departure lounge for Guatemala on my last leg of a tiring day of many flights. When I arrived at the lounge, I was the only visible minority and all of the signage and announcements were in Spanish. Equipped with only an English-Spanish dictionary, I was instantly thrust into my own "Oz" and was quite anxious about whether or not I was even in the right area of the airport (I was, and I am proud to say I made it to my destination). I mentally reminded myself that from that moment on I would be out of my element, that I would have to rely on myself, and that this was the type of experience and personal growth I had been seeking. On my return from Guatemala to North America, I was seated with an elderly Mayan lady who neither spoke nor understood English and who had obviously never traveled before. She was unaware of the need for a seat belt, and was unable to respond to flight attendants barking at her to put hers on, so I reached over and buckled it for her. At the customs and immigration checkpoint, back on American soil, my same elderly seatmate was in line ahead of me and clearly having much difficulty with the duty officers. For some reason the officers insisted on speaking English and were trying to get her to sign an X on a document, since she seemed unable to sign her name. I was struck by the fast-paced, assembly-line nature of our reentry into North America, of the impatience and callousness of certain personnel, and of the crowds, commercialism, and generic atmosphere. I recognized that I was becoming anxious, critical, and a bit angry and I now know that I was experiencing the first pangs of reverse culture shock. The familiar had now become a new "Oz."

Cate Carlyle, Nova Scotia, Canada

activist groups for issues you encountered).

- Connect with others who have been to the same locale, or who travel or work overseas.
- Ease back gradually into the usual busy pace; don't overdo it.
- Recognize that you have changed and will need time to readjust— don't make huge life decisions right away (career or personal).

Sharing Knowledge

Consider the following cliches: Two heads are better than one. It takes a village. Share and share alike. A problem shared is a problem halved. Returning from an international volunteer adventure and not sharing your knowledge and experience helps no one. By sharing what you have learned and experienced while away, you not only solidify your own takeaways and clarify any possible future goals and activities, but you can also enrich the lives, knowledge base, and skill set of those unable to take such journeys.

Shared Storytelling

WHAT DO YOU get when you put six librarians from six different countries into an intensive month-long program for professional and leadership development? Deep learning, deep friendships, and deep belly-filling laughter! While working in Singapore at Nanyang Technological University Libraries, I had the wonderful opportunity (twice) to deliver a long-standing professional development program to librarians from across Southeast Asia who had joined us for a one-month internship; the opportunities to learn from and with each other were tremendous. Though many initially attended the program hoping to learn from a more developed (and better-funded) library, participants soon experienced the power of shared storytelling and problem-solving among themselves. Librarians also soon learn that although their needs may be similar across university libraries, local practice often reveals great creativity and innovation. Personally, I have come away with rich relationships, both professional and personal, and a deep regard for what librarians can manage to achieve in often challenging settings. And then there are the memories of all that laughter, long and loud.

Dianne Cmor, Quebec, Canada

BROWN BAG LUNCH SESSION

One of the easiest ways for you to share your experience with your colleagues is to hold a brown bag lunch session when you return from your trip. Before leaving for an LWB Guatemala service trip, I approached my colleagues and asked them to donate funds that would be used for collection development at the Asturias Academy. Not only was this an easy way to raise $200 (which equaled more than 1,000 Guatemalan quetzals), but I felt accountable to record each dollar that was spent and show my colleagues the books they had purchased, and I knew a brown bag lunch session would be a great way to share this information. To my surprise, the turnout for my session was huge; it was standing room only! I spent an hour discussing the project work that we completed, the goals we achieved, and the fun that we had. Working as a volunteer in a school library teaching students literacy skills is similar to my work as an academic librarian, and my work at a university library teaching students information literacy and critical thinking skills. Both require an awareness of instructional and assessment strategies, and the ability to establish a good rapport with students, and both are most successful when shared with a community of practice.

No Books

WHILE WORKING IN Chajul, our team of volunteers shared their collective experience with a view to helping the librarians make decisions about the opportunities and difficulties which confront them. A masterful ruse by the local team is to tell the children that there are hidden cameras concealed around the library premises, in order to encourage the children to self-regulate their behavior within the library. My amusement was curtailed, however, by a chance comment by one of the local librarians in relation to theft; it occurs rarely and when it is detected, the librarians ask the child to explain why he or she stole from the library. It is sobering to hear that the response is usually "Because I love this book and I have none at home." I am accustomed to working in an environment which is so information-rich that it has to routinely destroy reading resources due to storage pressures, and so I was struck by the injustice of a child not having a single book of his or her own. This remains my most abiding memory of Guatemala, and rightly so.

Mairead Mooney, Ireland

WRITING

We believe that the experience of volunteering in a foreign library is a key component of international librarianship, and we also believe that making scholarly contributions to the profession is an important part of librarianship. Although the heart of our profession lies in helping people access the information they need and ensuring that information is preserved for future generations, actively participating in the cycle of knowledge creation has become increasingly important within our profession. Before, during, and after our first international volunteer trips, it was impossible for us to foresee that we would ever write a book on volunteering in international libraries. However, with each new volunteer adventure, we gained a wealth of experience that we eventually realized could be beneficial to other librarians considering similar adventures. The two of us have volunteered in libraries in Africa, Central America, and North America and we have visited libraries in Australia, the Caribbean, Europe, China, and throughout the United States and Canada. Needless to say, we are as passionate about traveling as we are about libraries and the amazing work done by librarians all over the world. Contributing to the LIS knowledge base is important, and any international work you conduct, whether paid or volunteer, is valuable to others in the profession. Writing articles for professional journals, blog posts, or web pages is an efficient way to share your experience and knowledge. This could include something as simple as writing for your association's newsletter, or your employer's intranet, to writing for a wider audience on open source sites or for international organizations such as the International Federation of Library Associations and Institutions.

Staying Connected After Your Trip

Ideally, your volunteer adventure will not end once you return home. The connections and partnerships you have made can continue to be of benefit to you, the host library, and future volunteers.

ONGOING ASSESSMENT

Continuous evaluation of the partnership's progress toward its goals is of critical importance to maintaining your relationship with a foreign library.

Technology has made it nearly effortless to coordinate meetings with colleagues around the globe, and we suggest using Skype, Google Hangouts, or Viber to check in with your partners at least semiannually (2–3 times a year). One of the first items on your agenda could be to review your current commitment, both to each other and to the programs, services, and resources being offered because of your collaboration:

- Is the partnership meeting its objectives?
- Is the partnership working well for both parties?
- What are its strengths and weaknesses?
- Can or should projects be reimagined, added, or retired?

It is important to establish measures to evaluate how well the volunteers are meeting the foreign library's objectives, and to review their effectiveness on an ongoing basis. Representatives of the organization that recruited the volunteers and of the library that hosted the volunteers should hold a debriefing session as soon as possible after each trip, to decide if the objectives were met, discuss the reasons they were or weren't met, identify successes

The Tangibles

I KNEW THE experience gained from leading a service trip would enrich my skills and create new professional development opportunities. I just didn't know how this would be manifested in a tangible form until maybe a few weeks after the trip. I'm currently developing a proposal to create a volunteer-based committee that explores the role of public libraries in contributing to civic engagement. It has become clear to me that there is a lot of interest from the public library community to support meaningful causes both locally and abroad. I hope to share my experience with my colleagues and develop a training course around social activism or civic engagement, while reflecting on my experiences. I'm also making presentations to committees and team meetings in my library, and I am raising awareness about and encouraging donations to the libraries I visited in Guatemala. My plans are to continue leading upcoming service trips for as long as the opportunity is there and my personal circumstances are favorable.

Jorge Rivera, Ontario, Canada

and challenges, and suggest revisions that should be made for future trips. Volunteers should also be asked to complete a survey that allows them to share their overall satisfaction with the trip and project work they participated in, comment on the trip organization, evaluate any training they may have received, and rate their satisfaction with accommodations and meals. If both partners are satisfied with the partnership, and all of your goals have been realized, you may want to consider establishing new goals and having volunteers assist from their home countries. For example, one activity that volunteers can accomplish from a distance is to help librarians and administrators apply for grants to purchase or maintain technology and software in their library.

KNOWLEDGE TRANSFER

Host libraries may also request a knowledge transfer outcome, or product, from the volunteer(s) after the service trip. One such product that is commonly requested is a toolkit. While toolkits can be concrete items stored in the library, in the context of international volunteer work, the toolkit will most likely be a large file composed of digital documents and links. The types of toolkits requested could include tools for implementing

- literacy programming
- community programming
- homework help programming
- conducting staff training and staff professional development
- fund-raising
- grant writing
- collection development
- donations policies

The volunteer LIS professional(s) may be asked to compile such a toolkit once they have time and then forward it to the host library for implementation. This can all be done online at a distance.

Another method of transferring knowledge that benefits both the host library and current and future volunteers is the creation of a volunteer handbook. This handbook can be created post-trip after having an opportunity to reflect, and then adjusted after consulting with the host library staff via e-mail or Skype. Such a handbook is important so that work done by LIS professionals (your work or others who volunteer) is maintained and continued. Unfortunately, sometimes well-meaning volunteers with no LIS background volunteer in international libraries with their social group, mission, or organization and can possibly undo important systems. For example, LIS volunteers may set up a cataloging and classification system for a host library. If there is no handbook or "how-to" guide available for continuing to implement this system, then when new items are added to the collection by new volunteers, the cataloging system may fall apart. A volunteer handbook will also be very useful for the host library when advertising for future volunteers. A handbook that includes systems in place, expectations, customs, and dress codes, for example, will ensure that applicants wishing to volunteer know what to expect and will be well matched with the host library.

Sample Toolkit Contents: Early Literacy Programming for Children

- Definition and overview of early literacy
- How to conduct community mapping
- Planning your programs
- Promoting your programs
- Training staff
- Working with families and community professionals
- Sample activities
- Resource lists (print and digital)
- Manipulatives
- Handouts
- Tools for evaluation and ongoing assessment
- Links to pertinent associations and community organizations

Maintaining Momentum

One priceless aspect of the experience of volunteering abroad is that you are instantly immersed in an intense environment with a group of like-minded people (librarians) from different places and with different life experiences. You may be a public librarian from Grandview Heights, Ohio, who is put on the same project team as a special librarian from Toronto, Ontario, and together you may be responsible for collaborating with a school librarian in Belize to implement a new cataloging system. This is an incredible opportunity that neither of you likely would have had in your usual workday routine, and the question you may ask yourself after returning home is "How can I continue to make a difference?" We understand that what you are really asking yourself is: how can I continue to feel a deep sense of professional purpose and accomplishment now that I'm back home?

Depending on the size of your professional network, you may have colleagues and students from multiple countries contact you and invite you to give an in-person or virtual lecture. Preparing and delivering a lecture can be extremely nerve-wracking, but since you're courageous enough to volunteer internationally (or at least strongly consider it), we know you can do it. If you don't know many people, but you're lucky enough to live in a city with a library school, you could contact the graduate program coordinator and pitch the idea of giving a special guest lecture on international librarianship that would be open to all library school students. If you present a well-received lecture and you're really feeling up for a challenge, you could submit a course proposal to design and teach an international librarianship course at your local iSchool. We know firsthand that teaching a university course is a lot of work, but we also know that it is incredibly rewarding and can renew your sense of passion for your regular professional work.

Another strategy is to always be on the lookout for opportunities to grow your network of professional volunteers. Keep in touch with the local librarians and other volunteers that you met on your trip. Make the effort to contact them and see if they have any new, interesting initiatives to consider. We once teamed up with two public librarians from Hamilton, Ontario, to present a session at the Ontario Library Association's Super Conference. Three out of four of the presenters had volunteered in international libraries—our numbers are growing! Once you've returned from your trip and had time to reflect, you may decide to blend your professional development and research interests by exploring the field of international and comparative librarianship from an academic perspective. Volunteering in different types of libraries, in different countries, or in vastly different regions in the same country will give you keen insights that are of interest to many in our profession. Don't be discouraged if nothing gets off the ground right away; sometimes opportunities take time to present themselves.

If you return home with a newfound appreciation for the familiar and routine, and have revised your plan to travel the world, you might consider channeling your interest in volunteerism into projects closer to home. If you find that you really benefited from the actual volunteer work, and not so much from the travel and adventure, then you can maintain that momentum by getting involved in local volunteer pursuits.

Advocacy

An advocate is someone who "supports or promotes the interests of a cause or group."[3] Depending on the country and organization in which you volunteered, you may feel that advocacy is needed once you are back on home soil; advocacy for the foreign library or institution itself, the community you temporarily called home, or the region or country you visited. Volunteering internationally may open your eyes to social, economic, political, or health issues in other countries, igniting a passion to advocate, fund-raise, or enlighten others. There are many advocacy initiatives you could facilitate once you return, from a simple, informal, round table-style "chat" to becoming involved in conference-style sessions, or to developing a course in international librarianship.

FOR THE INTERNATIONAL LIBRARY

Your host library will probably require some form of ongoing advocacy or fund-raising after your trip (hence the need for international volunteers to begin with), and you can advocate on the library's behalf in a number of ways, from simple to more complex events:

Simple:

- Talk about where you went, what you did, and why (informal conversations, elevator speeches) (see figure 6.1).
- Produce a display of your trip in your library to raise awareness.
- Conduct library programming based on your experience (a food class featuring the locale's cuisine, an informal travel session).
- Host Casual Friday fund-raising (make a donation to dress casually at work) or auction a signed copy of an author's work from the host country.

More effort:

- Host a documentary movie night or author talk focused on an issue, locale, or organization.
- Host a book drive or library book sale to raise funds.
- Present bake sales, cake walks, or auctions (literary-themed cake auctions are very popular).
- Host a "Book Face" contest among staff (taking pictures after lining up your profile with a book cover) that requires a small donation to enter.
- Conduct a conference-style presentation for your colleagues and library community (Skype-in the host library's staff, and feature experts on the local culture and any issues).

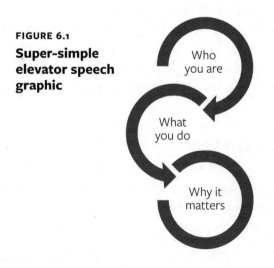

FIGURE 6.1

Super-simple elevator speech graphic

Who you are

What you do

Why it matters

Hard core:

- Stage a cultural gala or evening (food, music, entertainment high-lighting the locale visited).
- Partner with a local business or public entity related to the issue at hand (for example, partner with local clean water advocacy groups, or literacy or social justice groups to raise awareness about that issue in the host country).
- Solicit sponsorships from local businesses and philanthropists.
- If you've completed a DIY service trip, consider promoting and facilitating future service trips to the library on an ongoing basis.

FOR THE LIS PROFESSION

LIS professionals have an obligation to advocate for libraries and their profession. It is not enough to work in libraries and recognize their value, and then conceal all that greatness from the general public. *"At stake is both the very survival of libraries, as access points to information and ideas, and librarians, as organizers and deliverers of that information."*[4] We must spread the word about all that libraries have to offer and ensure their existence for generations to come. Once you have volunteered internationally, you are in a unique position to advocate for libraries and access to information globally. In doing so, you are serving as a global ambassador for the profession as a whole. You will have witnessed firsthand the need for access to information to empower citizens in less privileged or less connected societies, the need for Internet access and the elimination of the digital divide, and the need for trained professionals in LIS roles.

In the commercial world we often hear of "brand ambassadors," people hired to represent a company or product in an attractive light, increase the exposure of the brand, and increase sales. LIS professionals all have the ability to be brand ambassadors for our profession, not to bring about any increase in revenue, but to ensure the existence of libraries for the betterment of society. Libraries are not typically very visible institutions, and traditionally the preferred method of demonstrating their value has been through statistics: attendance, circulation, and revenue statistics. As an international library volunteer, I challenge you to champion our noble profession in more relevant and emotional ways. Talk about what you do, talk about where you visited and what is needed, talk about what libraries and LIS professionals have to offer, and talk about how libraries contribute to social capital. According to a Nielsen study of 28,000 global Internet users, 92 percent of people who responded say they trust recommendations from friends and family over any marketing in the mass media.[5]

Since "stories have an incredible power to distill human experience,"[6] tell the stories of your trip, of the positive changes you helped to bring about, of the lives you touched and those that touched you. Champion the LIS staff you worked with, and put a face on those countries and people that may be too far away for your friends and colleagues to ever meet or visit. Humanize those striving to make a change in the world, and spread the word about the role that libraries play in making those positive changes. Although your volunteer trip may have finished, the work to ensure the longevity of the LIS profession and of libraries around the world has not.

The end of a volunteer journey is not the end of your personal and professional journey. Keep the momentum going, and harness that newfound energy and commitment to your profession. Advocate, share, grow, give back, and continue to learn. You may not change someone else's life, but at the very least you have already changed your own.

Notes

1. "Reverse Culture Shock: The Challenges of Returning Home," U.S. State Department, 2017, https://www.state.gov/m/fsi/tc/c56075.htm.
2. Craig Storti, *The Art of Coming Home* (Maine: Intercultural, 2001).
3. *Merriam-Webster Dictionary*, 2017, https://www.merriam-webster.com/dictionary/advocate.
4. "Library Advocacy Now! A Training Program for Public Library Staff and Trustees," Canadian Association of Public Libraries, 2011, cla.ca/wp-content/uploads/LibraryAdvocacyNow.pdf.
5. "Consumer Trust in Online, Social, and Mobile Advertising Grows," Nielsen, 2012, www.nielsen.com/ca/en/insights/news/2012/consumer-trust-in-online-social-and-mobile-advertising-grows.html.
6. "Library Advocacy Now!"

chapter 7

Partner for Success
Collaborating with an International Library

IS THERE A COUNTRY OR CULTURE THAT FASCINATES YOU? DO YOU dream of visiting that area of the world and doing something to help with literacy efforts while there? I had long held an interest in the country of Guatemala, so when I saw a post on social medifira about a literacy volunteer opportunity there, I began working on my application immediately, not knowing what a major impact it would have on my life. I now travel to Guatemala annually with Librarians Without Borders (LWB) as the program manager for a local school library program. The advice in this chapter will help you have a successful experience in international library work, while giving you a heads-up about some of the challenges that you might encounter.

LWB was founded in 2005 by a group of librarians whose aim was to increase people's access to information resources in areas of the world where social and economic inequities existed. LWB's web page states that they want to do this by building sustainable libraries and by training and supporting library staff.[1]

In 2009, the Miguel Angel Asturias Academy in Quetzaltenango, Guatemala, asked LWB to assist in opening a school library. Most schools in Guatemala, as in most of Central America, do not have a school library. The founder and director of the school, Jorge Chojolán, was influenced heavily by

Paolo Freire's book *Pedagogy of the Oppressed*. In his book, Freire argues that for oppressed people to become liberated from their oppressors, they must become intimately involved in their own education. Freire, who worked as an adult literacy instructor in Brazil, believed that literacy and critical thinking are crucial for oppressed people to break free of their oppression.[2] Guatemala's indigenous community has experienced much oppression at the hands of Spaniards and the authoritarian governments that followed. Chojolán designed the curriculum of the school around thematic units that encourage the students to think critically about their world and to challenge existing prejudices in their society, with the hope that the next generation of leaders will create a more level playing field for all.

Asturias Academy is a private, nonprofit K–12 school that offers subsidized tuition and scholarships to students with financial need. The school serves approximately 200 students who come from many backgrounds: indigenous, non-indigenous, poor, and middle class. Approximately 50 percent of the population in the city of Quetzaltenango is indigenous Maya.[3] The school teaches its students to take pride in their indigenous background and reinforces that pride by teaching all students to speak basic K'iche', an indigenous Mayan language spoken in that region. To promote equality among the sexes, all children, including boys, take sewing classes and all children, including girls, take woodworking classes.

The founders of LWB assisted the Asturias Academy with its dream of opening a school library. Construction began in 2010 and was completed in 2011, the same year that a group of LWB volunteers visited the school to donate, catalog, and process new books, arrange the books on the shelves, and brainstorm programming ideas with school staff. Each year, groups of volunteers visit the school to further the library program.

Keys to Running a Successful Program

My trips to Guatemala have taught me that to foster a successful partnership, you must have

- a team focus
- humility

- regular communication
- good listening skills
- follow-through
- flexibility

FOCUS ON THE TEAM

If you're a librarian who likes to travel, going on an international library trip might sound like a great adventure, but it's not all about the travel. You have to work well with others in order for your efforts to have a positive impact. As one international librarian noted, "Being a well-traveled library professional does not necessarily qualify one as an appropriate cultural fit. Experience working with others, flexibility, and demonstrated team-building skills help ensure continued success."[4] LWB runs a service trip to Guatemala every year and recruits volunteers to work at the Asturias Academy. Potential volunteers apply to serve on the team and, if selected, receive training on the history of the school, expectations for the trip, and cultural awareness issues. Volunteers need to have a heart for people, be flexible, and be good team players. Helping other team members with emotional support is more important than having travel experience. This is especially true when things don't go as planned, such as when team members fall ill.

If you're planning on working with other volunteers, consider breaking up into smaller groups. LWB places its volunteers on different teams. The library Programming Team plans and conducts fun literacy programs for students in kindergarten through ninth grade. Groups conduct programs such as puppet shows, skits, songs, dances, and readers' theater for the children. Groups often plan a craft or other hands-on activity that relates to the theme of the program. Resources such as puppets, a puppet stage, craft supplies, and other teaching materials are left at the school for the teachers and librarian to use in the future.

Another team of volunteers works on collection development for the library. The school does not have any funds for purchasing books, and relies on donations from partner organizations and donors to fill its bookshelves. LWB receives monetary donations that allow the trip leaders to purchase materials for the school. Many volunteers purchase books with their personal funds and seek donations from friends and family to donate to the school.

Once in Guatemala City, service trip participants visit a local publisher to purchase books. We try to purchase as many books as possible in Guatemala because the books are relevant to the children's culture, are written in Guatemalan Spanish, and help the local economy. Purchasing books locally supports the writers, illustrators, editors, small presses, and everyone else involved in the publishing process.

In addition to providing books for pleasure reading, a school library also needs to provide books that support the curriculum. Volunteers conduct a teacher survey every year to ascertain the curriculum needs for the school. Those requests are shared with volunteers and donors, who prioritize their purchases based on the stated needs.

The Collection Development team processes, catalogs, and adds books to the library's collection. Volunteers receive training on the cataloging process before the service trip, but once on the ground, teamwork and creativity are needed to organize the team and the process. The library uses the Dewey Decimal classification system for its nonfiction books and classifies its fiction books into three categories—picture books, early chapter books, and advanced fiction. The library's holdings are saved onto an Excel spreadsheet, which also stores the student information that is needed to check out books.

In 2015, LWB started providing teacher training during the annual service trip. The trainings have focused on developing information literacy skills, incorporating books into lessons, using books in math and science classes, improving student reading comprehension, and early literacy.

The collaboration between the organizations has led to the program's success. The vision for the library, the planning for the space, the books being added to the collection, the programming, and the teacher trainings have all been a result of collaborating and planning together. LWB asks lots of questions, the school communicates its needs, we brainstorm together, select a course of action together, and move forward from there. Even the schedule and tourist activities for the trip's participants are planned together, balancing the needs of the school with feedback from previous years' participants.

BE HUMBLE

It is important to embark on a relationship with an international partner with humility. Too often, people from North America see themselves as the givers of knowledge and focus only on the deficits of the community they want to serve. Every area of the world has its own strengths, and we need to celebrate those, building programs around them. The people in the community know the language, the culture, their own needs, and how to reach the target audience. They will have a good understanding of what will work and how to approach problems. They will know the potential obstacles and how to avoid them. LWB strives to work in partnership with the Asturias Academy, avoiding a colonizing relationship, one which Freire referred to as "cultural invasion," "with the invader assuming the role of a helping friend."[5] We want to avoid going into the relationship with our own objectives, without truly listening to the needs of the people. This can be done by building our programs around the community's strengths and admitting that we don't know everything.

Book selection is an area where we need to practice humility. When selecting books, LWB volunteers consider carefully whether the story line or illustrations would make sense to someone from the rural countryside in Guatemala. Many Guatemalan children do live in cities and can relate to stories with an urban setting, but the goal is to provide a diversity of materials, not just a Western, Caucasian perspective on everyday life. Books sold in North America often have settings that might be unfamiliar to the children, and their story lines and plots are too far removed from the experiences of children in Guatemala.

COMMUNICATE REGULARLY

In any relationship, good communication is crucial, and the same is true for two partner organizations. Stay connected with your partner library through e-mail, online meetings, and social media. It's important to communicate regularly, even if it's just a short message through Facebook. I also remain connected by staying current on news from the area so that if something happens, I can check in on our friends in Guatemala. This sends the very real message that we care and are concerned for them. After the media in your country has forgotten about events in your partner's country, check in on them and ask for a follow-up.

Has your partner's staff shared personal stories or concerns, such as health issues or stories about their children? When you check in with them, ask how they're doing with that health issue, that problem at school, or how their children are doing. I also like to read about the history of Guatemala, but when I'm there, I ask questions about what I've read and then ask the people there to tell me about it. They are more than happy to tell me their perspective, and that's when I receive the real history lesson. People like to be heard and like to know that you're interested in their country and their lives.

LISTEN

Being a good listener will lead to a great relationship. Listen in order to understand your partner's needs, ask how you can help fill those needs, and then follow through on what you promised. The idea for children's programming in the Asturias library originated when our volunteers listened to our partner's explanation for the lack of literacy experiences in Guatemala. Books are expensive relative to a worker's salary, so few people have books in the home. There are few public libraries in Guatemala, so most children and teachers don't have any experience with library story times or programs. The library programs that LWB conducts at Asturias serve not only to make the library and literacy fun for the students, but also provide an opportunity to model effective, sustainable programs for the teachers and librarian. As much as possible, we try to connect our library programs to the thematic unit that the children are studying that month.

What is the history of your partner organization? What are its core values? Once you know what is important to your partners, you can plan programs that fit within that framework. By listening to Chojolán's story of his inspiration for the creation of the school, the LWB librarians knew how important Freire's ideas were to him, so we went into the relationship knowing that we had to work with the people in the school and not just for them. We listen carefully to their needs, brainstorm how we can help them fill those needs, and then problem-solve together.

Some needs might not be obvious to you, but if you listen to your partner, you'll understand the culture better and can then help fill those needs.

In Guatemala, families living at the poverty level would need to save two or three days' worth of wages to purchase an average-priced book. Approximately half of Guatemala's people live in poverty, resulting in many families living without books in the home.[6] Many Guatemalan teachers grew up without access to books and don't have books or libraries in their schools, making it difficult for them to know how to use books in the classroom. For these reasons, Chojolán asked LWB to provide training for the teachers that would demonstrate how to incorporate books into their lessons. We might never have known on our own that this was a need. The topics for the workshops are suggested by Chojolán and the teachers themselves. At the end of every training, the teachers provide us with feedback, including ideas for future workshops and suggestions for books and resources that they need in the library and in their classrooms.

FOLLOW THROUGH

To be considered reliable, you need to follow through on your promises. Be honest in what you can deliver. If you foresee difficulties, let your partner know. When we ask for feedback from the teachers, we read their comments and use them to plan our next trainings. When the teachers make requests for books, we respond by making those needs known to our donors and pur-

The Asturias Academy Perspective

THE SUPPORT OF Librarians Without Borders is valuable for our school, since the library is a very important bastion for the education that this institution offers to its students.

The training of teachers and parents has yielded positive results, which we see both in the performance and in the interest in reading in the majority of students. This year, the number of students in elementary and secondary grades who attended the library in order to borrow books has increased.

We appreciate that Librarians Without Borders is interested in solving our needs and in what the library and the teachers need to provide a better education to the students.

Dora A. Domínguez Piedrasanta, Xela, Guatemala

chasing the books and materials requested. Because we follow through on our plans and respond to their requests, a relationship of trust has developed. The teachers feel comfortable asking us questions and giving honest feedback.

A strong, trusting relationship is key to building a successful partnership, and following through on your promises will help develop trust. I was present during a difficult faculty meeting at Asturias one spring when the director asked every teacher for his or her opinion. I did not expect to be included in the process and was not commenting on the situation, which I felt was for them to discuss and problem-solve. When the director asked for my opinion too, I felt both honored and humbled that I was considered one of the staff and that he valued my opinion. If they had not trusted me, I would not even have been invited to be present during that meeting.

BE FLEXIBLE

Good programs change over time to adjust to current needs. LWB's partnership with the Asturias Academy has evolved over the years to reflect the needs of the school. It took several years to build the library's collection and implement the right software and hardware in order to begin lending books. For the first few years, students browsed the collection during school hours and used the books in-house. Students and teachers were given library orientations and were taught library skills, such as how to use a shelf marker and how the collection's sections were organized. Many students had never held a book in their hands and had to be taught how to turn the pages and care for a book. Beginning in 2014, the school started allowing students to check out books overnight. Because children's books are difficult to acquire and there are no funds to replace lost or damaged books, the school took a big risk in allowing students to borrow books. The librarian continues to train children on caring for books, and she places each child's book in a plastic bag to minimize damage to it. Some books do get lost or damaged, and because many of the children's families cannot afford to pay the replacement cost of a book, children are given the option to work off their charges in the library. The students and parents have now become accustomed to the idea of a lending library and have begun asking for longer checkout periods.

You might find yourself getting comfortable with the programs that you're offering your partner. Take a risk! Add new programs and then adjust them, according to needs. The training that we conduct is another example of a program that has evolved. It can be difficult to find librarians willing to serve on a trip who are comfortable conducting teacher workshops, especially in another language. The first year that we conducted a teacher workshop, the training was planned in English, with on-the-spot translating being conducted by several Spanish-speaking participants. Translating educational and literacy terms was mentally exhausting for the translators. Furthermore, lots of time was spent presenting in English, which the teachers did not understand. The following year, translations were done before the trip, and the workshop was presented in Spanish, resulting in more time spent on the topic rather than on translating. Subsequent workshops have followed the same pattern—planning well in advance and translating materials into Spanish before the trip, with the training delivered in Spanish.

Toss around new ideas and see if your partner thinks they will work. Early literacy is a topic not often discussed in Guatemala, but when our groups briefly touched on early literacy topics in some of the trainings, the teachers and school director found the topic fascinating. The trainings have now evolved to include parent trainings. Recently, I arrived in Guatemala a few days before the rest of the participants in order to conduct early literacy training for the parents of young children in the school. The topic was so popular that a second session had to be added in the afternoon. The training was conducted after an informational parent meeting, and although it was not required, most of the families stayed for the training. I used the Public Library Association's Every Child Ready to Read materials in Spanish for the bulk of the content, but I inserted information about early brain development. I also changed most of the photos in the slide show, which showed too many Anglo families in North American settings to work well in Guatemala, where people are darker-skinned, dress differently than North Americans, and are more likely to live in a rural setting. After the workshop, each family received a free book to take home. Our long-term goal is to create a culture of literacy that begins in the home.

Do what you can to make your programs sustainable. The day before the parent workshop, I conducted a more in-depth early literacy workshop with the teachers. They were thrilled with the training and commented that nothing like this was being taught to parents and teachers in Guatemala. Chojolán hopes to continue offering early literacy workshops to parents, with the workshops being delivered by Asturias Academy teachers.

Parent Training

AN ASTURIAS ACADEMY
parent's comment: "Es un taller muy bueno que nos ayuda mucho como padres."
  Translation: "This is a good workshop that helps us as parents."

As the teachers have received more training, their requests for materials have changed too. They have learned methods to incorporate books into their lessons and have begun to request more nonfiction books to support their science lessons, and graphic novels to encourage reluctant readers to pick up a book. Teachers are also requesting training on how to differentiate their instruction for students with special needs and students who are reading below grade level.

The close relationship and flexibility we enjoy with the school has also allowed us volunteers to connect students in the United States with students in Guatemala. Several times, students in Virginia and Texas have written letters and corresponded with students at Asturias. I delivered pen pal letters from Guatemala to a class of Spanish students in Texas and enjoyed seeing their excitement in receiving replies to their letters. One student told me that it was the highlight of his year in Spanish class.

Last year, we connected students by setting up an online meeting. A middle school Spanish class in Texas held a video conference with a middle school class at Asturias. The classes took turns asking each other questions about their lives, their school, and their country. The classes erupted in cheers when they discovered that both classes' favorite food was pizza! We could not have provided this unique opportunity for the students if we and the teachers had not been flexible with schedules and were not creative problem-solvers with technology.

Be flexible with your plans, because nothing ever goes exactly according to plan. Mishaps happen; flights get delayed, someone always gets sick, and sometimes the weather doesn't cooperate. Sometimes you have to change your plans or scrap them altogether. Safety takes priority, so even if you don't do everything that you intended to do, you should do what is necessary to remain safe. During one trip, part of our group stayed the night in a different city than planned because of protests planned against the government the following day that were going to shut down major roadways. Many of us had flights scheduled to leave the next day, so we decided to stay the night near the airport in case the roads were shut down. In the worst-case scenario, we would at least be able to walk to the airport. Being flexible with our plans made the experience go much more smoothly than if we had attempted to adhere to our schedule.

Challenges and Solutions

No matter how well you plan, there will always be some snags. The following are some of the challenges that we've encountered, along with advice on how to get around those hurdles.

COMMUNICATING

For your partnership to be successful, you need to communicate efficiently and regularly. This can be difficult if you don't speak the language of your partners, so try to find someone who does speak it and is willing to help you. In the early days of LWB, few volunteers spoke Spanish well enough to communicate directly with the school director. Conversations and e-mails had to be translated, which slowed down communication. Having a program manager who speaks Spanish fluently has facilitated the communication process greatly. While speaking Spanish is not required for volunteers on the service trip, having a few volunteers who know the language makes for more efficient communication once the group is in Guatemala. This helps in many ways, from ordering food at restaurants and reading street signs to asking the school staff questions directly and talking with the students.

Remaining in contact throughout the year can be a challenge if your partner organization has Internet problems. Skype meetings can be delayed or end early if there is a connectivity issue. It can take several days to get a reply to an e-mail if the school is having Internet problems. Practice patience and keep trying to communicate. When in another country, spotty Wi-Fi can also make it difficult to communicate back home. Many of us have learned to find cafés and restaurants with reliable Internet connections to contact our family back home, post on social media, and check e-mails.

TRANSPORTING MATERIALS

If you are taking donated items to another country, you'll have to figure out how to transport those materials. Can you ship the items with a large shipping company? How much will they charge? What does it take to get them through Customs? Do you need a special note stating that they are being donated to a school or library? Can you purchase items in your partner's home country instead? Purchasing items there will help the local economy, give your partner more culturally relevant materials, and free you of the headache of transporting items there.

Our organization has chosen to transport donations by packing them in participants' luggage rather than pay exorbitant shipping fees. We strive to purchase as many of our donations as possible in Guatemala, but there are

Oops!

EVEN WHEN WE know the language, words can have different meanings in different countries. Sometimes this causes embarrassing communication problems, such as when I used the Mexican Spanish word for "drinking straw" (*popote*), which in Guatemalan Spanish means "big poop." When I used the word to demonstrate steps for a craft, the students started giggling. They wouldn't tell me why they were giggling, so I finally asked the librarian, who explained what popote meant in Guatemala. I laughed and asked her to teach me their word for "straw," which is pajilla.

Debbie Chavez, Texas, U.S.A.

some resources that are simply not available there. We add a few hundred items to one library's collection each year, so for the time being, carrying books in our luggage is working, though cumbersome. It can be difficult to haul books in luggage, trying not to exceed the weight limits set by airlines and pulling the heavy luggage around airports.

If you choose to ship larger quantities of materials such as books, shipping costs can be prohibitive, so seek outside donors that can sponsor the shipping. If you do ship items, what will it take to get those items to your partner? In our case, even if we shipped books to Guatemala, shipping companies only deliver to Guatemala City. A school staff member would then bear the burden of traveling five hours to the capital to pick up the shipment. LWB strives to give in a way that does not burden the school.

FINDING THE RIGHT BOOKS

If you plan on donating books to people in another country, be careful about what you donate. Sometimes well-intentioned people donate the wrong kinds of books to the school that we partner with. LWB volunteers receive guidance on book selection, but the school works with other organizations as well. Foreign visitors sometimes donate books that cannot be used at the school, but the staff at Asturias want to be respectful and appreciative, and so they choose not to reject donations. For example, books have been donated that are written in English. While the school does teach English to the older students, a picture book in English will go largely unused. The librarian at Asturias, Señora Dorita, has asked our Spanish-speaking volunteers in the past to translate those books into Spanish, attaching the translation on a Post-it note on each page so that the teachers can read it to their students. It is better to donate only the types of books that are needed, so that you don't burden your partner with unusable materials.

Take care that you're not imposing the cultural values and traditions of your country on the people that you're working with. If people are donating books and other materials to your cause, go through each donated item to ensure that it's culturally relevant. For example, the children at Asturias love Clifford the Big Red Dog books by Norman Bridwell, but a book that has Clifford hunting for Easter eggs might not resonate with children in Guatemala, where Easter remains a largely religious holiday. Because U.S. culture is well known around the world, children may have heard about Easter egg hunts, but by sending books filled with North American traditions and customs, volunteers risk imposing their culture and traditions on the children.

Make every effort to find books that your partner has requested, even when this is difficult. The teachers at Asturias have requested more nonfiction books for the library so that they can weave the books into the science curriculum. We attempt to purchase as many books as possible in Guatemala, but there are few nonfiction books for children and teens being published there. As a result, many of the nonfiction books that we donate are purchased in North America, which brings with it the challenge of not purchasing books that are too centered on Anglo culture. Some possible solutions to this challenge include attending local book fairs and purchasing from publishers located in nearby countries.

Try to find books and other resources in the local indigenous languages, too. Because the Asturias Academy teaches K'iche' to the students, the teachers are eager to acquire books written in that language. The school has managed to locate some titles, but finding books written in indigenous languages is a challenge. Contact other nonprofit agencies working in that country to see if they have self-published any materials in local indigenous languages.

MANAGING TIME

Lastly, you will most likely find that there never seems to be enough time to accomplish everything that you would like. On one of our trips the librarian, Señora Dorita, asked us to help her inventory the library collection. She was frustrated that the catalog didn't accurately reflect what was on the shelves. Unfortunately, because of volunteer illnesses and other setbacks, we were unable to conduct the inventory. Because we only visit the school once a year, I was disappointed that we were not able to help her with this request. It would be ideal to make more visits throughout the year, but we have our lives, our work, and our families that need our attention back home. Work with your partner to prioritize projects, do as much as you can with the time that you have, and consider recruiting more volunteers to help you accomplish your goals. You may not be able to help them pay for their costs, but there are people willing to pay for the trip themselves in order to reap the personal benefits of volunteering with you.

Why You'll Want to Keep Going Back

Librarians working in international librarianship often find that the best part of the experience is the new friendships they make. You'll forget all about the uncomfortable showers you might have endured, but you will remember your new friends. You might meet other librarians who work in a different type of library than you do. You might meet someone from your same state and get together regularly after your trip. You might hit it off well with someone from the country where you volunteered and remain in contact through social media.

The new friendships that I have formed are the most cherished piece of my work. The people that I have met in Guatemala are beautiful, accepting, and loving. They have welcomed me into their classrooms, their libraries, and their city. They have served me delicious meals, watched over our groups when we've toured their city, and made themselves vulnerable by recounting very personal stories. The students have hugged and kissed me and invited us to play tag at recess and soccer after school. I stay in touch with some of the school staff through social media. I think about them and worry about them just like I do my friends and family back home. You'll find your heart expanding to make room for your new friends.

Another benefit is the education and professional development that you will receive. Many librarians in North America have never seen a library in another country. We assume that libraries are somewhat similar around the world. When I visited a library in my grandmother's hometown in Mexico in the 1990s, I realized how different their libraries are when I found that my collection of children's books at home was much larger than the library's entire collection of books. I was also shocked when I visited public libraries in Guatemala and learned that the stacks were closed to patrons and the collections did not circulate. These observations helped me become a better librarian in the United States, where I served many refugees and other immigrants in a public library setting. When giving library orientations to these groups, I always started at the very beginning with how libraries in the United States differ from libraries around the world, and I would demonstrate the services and resources that our library offered.

You will also find that you come away having learned a lot about the history of the area that you visit. Even if you're not a history buff, being present in that country will make that place's history more interesting and bring it to life. You'll learn how the country's history informs current situations that you may not have understood before. You will also learn about the geography and natural landscape. I have been awed by the natural beauty of Guatemala when hiking in mystical rain forests and swimming in the jade-colored water of hot springs. I am now much more aware of politics, popular music, and natural disasters in the region, which I hope makes me a better global citizen. You'll become a storyteller, and your friends, family, and coworkers will become more aware of what people in other parts of the globe experience, which can sometimes result in donations to your project.

You will experience a personal satisfaction that is immeasurable. When I go to Guatemala every spring, I feel as if I am visiting family, and the hugs and smiles that I receive from the teachers and students show me that they feel the same. One of the best decisions of my life was choosing to become involved in international library work. The people of Guatemala have shown me a different way of looking at the world, and I am thankful that I embarked on this journey.

By engaging in international librarianship, I have found a field of endeavor that allows me to combine all of my interests, strengths, and skills: my passion for helping people, my love of teaching, my love of reading and books, and my Spanish-language skills. My hope is that you also find your passion, perhaps as an international librarian.

Debbie Chavez is a school librarian with the Round Rock Independent School District in the Austin, Texas, area. She serves as the program manager of the Asturias school library program in Guatemala with Librarians Without Borders. Chavez has worked with refugee and other immigrant populations and on early literacy programs with the Pima County Public Library in Tucson, Arizona. Check out her blog at debchavez blog.wordpress.com.

Notes

1. Librarians Without Borders, 2017, www.lwb-online.org.

2. Paolo Freire, *Pedagogy of the Oppressed* (1970; New York: Continuum International, 2000), 48, 122–24.

3. Instituto Nacional de Estadística Guatemala, Gobierno de Guatemala, "Caracterización República de Guatemala," 2014, https://www.ine.gob.gt/sistema/uploads/2014/02/26/L5pNHMXzxy5FFWmk9NHCrK9x7E5Qqvvy.pdf.

4. Sandra Kendall, "The Toronto-Addis Ababa Academic Collaboration Library Science Program: A Case Study in Global Librarianship in Ethiopia," in *International Librarianship: Developing Professional, Intercultural, and Educational Leadership*, ed. Constantia Constantinou, Michael J. Miller, and Kenneth Schlesinger (New York: State University of New York Press, 2016), 3–14.

5. Freire, *Pedagogy of the Oppressed*, 52–53.

6. Instituto Nacional de Estadística Guatemala, Gobierno de Guatemala, "Caracterización República de Guatemala," 14.

chapter 8

Do Your Homework
Online Resources to Get You Started

A wise man will make more opportunities than he finds.
—Francis Bacon

INTERNET RESOURCES ARE FLUID AND CHANGE BY THE MINUTE, SO it is impossible to create a permanent and complete resource list. Blogs come and go, organizations appear and disband, and service trips may run annually or be one-time affairs. The resource list in this chapter reflects blogs, discussion lists, donation programs, and travel opportunities and organizations pertaining to volunteering and international libraries that were active and available at the time of writing. Online searches should not be limited to "library" opportunities, but should include all aspects of LIS skill sets and transferable skills: literacy, education, teaching, reading, information, community development, English as a new language, English as a second language (ESL), English as an additional language (EAL), English-language learning (ELL), and Internet technology.

Online Resources

LIS professionals are adept at finding information online, and therefore this resource list is just a jumping-off point and by no means a comprehensive list. Some of the organizations' websites featured here have links to other chapters or branches that might be useful in a search for volunteer opportunities. Those groups hosting annual trips may change their locale from year to year, so it is advisable to consult these links frequently for the most current information or to add yourself to any applicable organization's e-mail list.

Blogs

Go Abroad: LIS Internships Abroad

https://www.goabroad.com/intern-abroad/search/library-info-science/internships-abroad

> This is an online resource for international travel in various disciplines, including LIS. It includes links to travel guides, reviews, program opportunities, internships, scholarships, and partnerships.

International Librarians Network (ILN)

http://interlibnet.org

> The ILN hosts a blog pertaining to peer mentorship and international librarianship.

International Relations Round Table (IRRT)

www.ala.org/irrt/

> The IRRT is a membership unit of the American Library Association with publications on international librarianship, presentations, mentoring and hosting of international visitors and staff, and resource development and guidelines.

The Traveling Librarian

https://sarahpgibson.wordpress.com

> International librarian Sarah P. Gibson's blog provides links to both volunteer and employment postings from various associations and employers.

Book Donation Programs

African Library Project: *www.africanlibraryproject.org*

Better World Books: *https://www.betterworldbooks.com*

Biblionef: *http://biblionef.fr*

Book Aid International: *https://www.bookaid.org*

Books for Africa: *https://www.booksforafrica.org*

Bridge to Asia: *www.bridge.org*

Canadian Organization for Development through Education (CODE): *www.codecan.org*

Canadian School Book Exchange: *https://csbe.net/routingPages/AllDonations.aspx*

Darien Book Aid Plan: *www.darienbookaid.org*

International Board on Books for Young People (IBBY): *www.ibby.org*

International Book Project: *www.intlbookproject.org*

Discussion Lists

ACRL-AAME[1]

This moderated list supports activities related to membership in the Association of College and Research Libraries' Asian, African, and Middle Eastern Section, which promotes better communication between the members and the executive committee.

To Subscribe: Send the message *subscribe AAMES-L* followed by your name to listproc@ala.org.

ALA-WORLD

This discussion list is for the American Library Association's International Relations Round Table.

To Subscribe: Send the message *subscribe alaworld* followed by your name to listproc@ala.org.

ALCASALIST: Africana Librarians Council (ALC) of the United States

This discussion list is for the African Studies Association.

To Subscribe (for ALC members only): alcasalist@lists.stanford.edu.

APALA

This discussion list is for the Asia/Pacific American Librarians Association (APALA).

To Subscribe (for APALA members only): Send the message *subscribe apala-1* followed by your name to listserv@listserv.uic.edu.

CALA

This discussion list is for the Chinese American Librarians Association (CALA).

To Subscribe: Leave the subject line blank. Send the message *subscribe cala* followed by your name to listserv@csd.uwm.edu.

IFLA-L

This electronic forum is intended to foster communications between the International Federation of Library Associations and Institutions, its membership, and members of the international library community. The goal in establishing this list is to facilitate information exchange as well as professional communication and development within the IFLA community. The archives are available at *http://infoserv.inist.fr/wwsympa.fcgi/arc/ifla-1.*

To Subscribe: E-mail ifla.listserv@infoserv.inist.fr or use the web interface. If you subscribe by e-mail, in the body of the message type: "subscribe IFLA-L YourFirstname YourLastname" (without the quotes). To submit to the list, e-mail ifla-1 @infoserv.inist.fr.

ILIGlist-Discussion Group

The ILIGlist is an e-mail discussion group run by, and primarily for, International Library and Information Group (ILIG) members of the Chartered Institute of Library and Information Professionals. However, it welcomes non-ILIG members who are involved in LIS activities anywhere in the world.

To Subscribe: For more information, visit the International Library and Information Group website.

LALA-L (Latin Americanist Librarians' Announcements List)

This discussion list is for the Seminar on the Acquisition of Latin American Library Materials (SALALM). Membership in SALALM is required for enrollment.

To Subscribe (for SALALM members only): Contact gwilliam@arches.uga
.edu.

LIBJOBS

This IFLA mailing list is for librarians and information professionals
who are seeking employment. Subscribers receive only job postings. The
archives are available at http://infoserv.inist.fr/wwsympa.fcgi/arc/libjobs.

To Subscribe: E-mail ifla.listserv@infoserv.inist.fr or use the web interface.

MELANET-L

This is the discussion list of the Middle East Librarians Association
(MELA).

To Subscribe: Use the online form at http://mela.us/melanet.html or send a
message to listowner@mela.us requesting to be added to the list.

SLAVLIB

This discussion list is for Slavic and Eastern European librarians and archi-
vists, those in libraries responsible for Slavic collections, and LIS students
who are interested in pursuing careers in Slavic libraries.

To Subscribe: For information, e-mail Sandra Levy at slevy@uchicago
.edu requesting to be added to the list.

WESS-Discussion Groups

The Western European Studies Section (WESS) discussion list has regular
discussion groups for European Studies librarians.

To Subscribe: For more information, visit the WESS Discussion Groups web
page.

Service Trips

*Trip descriptions are taken from each organization's website.

$ = Denotes a fee required, usually to cover food and lodging, or as a donation, or just to participate. Flights to the destination country are rarely, if ever, included in the fee.

African Library Project (via Peace Corps)

www.africanlibraryproject.org/

The African Library Project coordinates book drives in the United States and partners with African schools and villages to start small libraries.

$ American Library Association (ALA) Cuba Tour

www.ala.org/aboutala/offices/ala-havana-book-fair-tour

In addition to the Havana Book Fair and the unique sights and sounds of Cuba, this annual tour features a half-day professional program with Cuban colleagues and a library volunteering opportunity to assist a library in need.

Apple Tree Library (China)

www.appletreelibrary.org/

This program promotes reading and builds English-language capacity in China, through public/private U.S./China collaborations to establish public children's libraries. It offers opportunities to volunteer, donate funds, donate books, and adopt a library.

$ Bamboo

https://www.wearebamboo.com/volunteer/program.php

Bamboo currently works with over thirty projects in countries such as Thailand, Cambodia, Nepal, Vietnam, Ethiopia, Rwanda, Costa Rica, Peru, and more. Project types vary massively from teaching English to installing water purification systems.

BiblioWorks (Bolivia)

http://biblioworks.org

BiblioWorks is a nonprofit organization that promotes literacy and education. Its mission is to provide communities with tools and resources to develop sustainable literacy and educational programs through schools, libraries, and cultural institutions. Volunteers work directly with communities in need in Bolivia.

$ The Book Bus

www.thebookbus.org/index.html

>The Book Bus works to improve child literacy rates in Africa, Asia, and South America by providing children with books and the inspiration to read them. Enthusiastic volunteers who love children and story times are needed to help deliver children's programming.

$ Canadian Alliance for Development Initiatives and Projects (CADIP)

www.cadip.org/index

>This nonprofit Canadian organization has no religious or political affiliation. Through various charity and volunteer initiatives, CADIP promotes peace, cooperation, tolerance, and understanding in multicultural, multiethnic, and international surroundings. The organization also promotes patterns and examples of civil activities focused on serving others, on building social ties and strengthening communities, and on supporting civil society development. Opportunities are available to manage a library and promote reading in Togo.

Ethiopia Reads

https://www.ethiopiareads.org/

>Ethiopia Reads was established in 1998 and has started seventy-two libraries to date. It works to ensure access to library materials, offers after-school programs, and supports library managers by providing them with professional development.

Frontiers Foundation (Operation Beaver)

www.frontiersfoundation.ca/volunteer

>Frontiers Foundation is a Canadian aboriginal nonprofit organization that promotes the advancement of economically and socially disadvantaged communities. The Operation Beaver Program focuses on providing affordable housing and improvements in education. With the support of government and charitable donations, both from the private sector and individuals, the program operates within Canadian borders, and overseas. Long-term opportunities are available in schools and school libraries. Travel costs in country, living and insurance costs, and winter clothing are covered with three- to ten-month commitments.

$ Globe Aware: Adventures in Service (Vietnam, Portable Mobile Libraries Projects)

http://globeaware.org/destinations/asia/vietnam

>This is a nonprofit whose short-term volunteer programs in international

environments encourage people to immerse themselves in a unique way of giving back. It offers "volunteer vacations."

$ Global Volunteers (Volunteer vacations-Cook Islands, organizing libraries)

https://globalvolunteers.org/cook-islands

This offers volunteer vacations that focus on worldwide community development projects.

$ Go for Hope (Nicaragua)

www.goforhope.org

Go for Hope International is a nonprofit educational organization that exists to support the development of children's libraries throughout Nicaragua. Through donations, pen pal programs, and service-learning trips, the organization provides funding, books, resources, and other support to improve educational outcomes for the children of Nicaragua.

Hester J. Hodgdon Libraries for All Program in Central America

www.librariesforall.org/volunteers

The Hester J. Hodgdon Libraries for All Program is a Colorado-based, tax-exempt, charitable foundation established in 2003 to support the San Juan del Sur Biblioteca in Nicaragua and to promote lending libraries in Central America. Help is welcome in many capacities, from working with technical systems in the library, to teaching a class, to painting faces at special library events.

$ Librarians Without Borders (LWB)

http://lwb-online.org

LWB has been running library service trips to Guatemala annually since 2010. This is a great opportunity to work hands-on in library development projects while building strong international connections. LWB was created and is governed by LIS professionals in North America.

Open Windows Foundation

www.openwindowsfoundation.com

The Open Windows Foundation's Learning Center has a reading room with over 10,000 books. Volunteers need to know basic Spanish, and their project work is customized to their skill set and could include listening to children read, helping students with their homework, or developing and implementing instructional workshops.

$ Operation Groundswell

http://operationgroundswell.com

> This is an immersive "backpackitivist" experience. Operation Groundswell has created partnerships with local charities, community leaders, and local governments in order to build a program that combines community service with an educational program that teaches team members the context needed to understand local challenges before solving them.

$ Supporting Kids in Peru (SKIP)

https://skipperu.org

> SKIP is a nonprofit organization that helps economically disadvantaged children in El Porvenir realize their right to an education. SKIP is currently working on the north coast of Peru, in the impoverished districts that surround the city of Trujillo. Short- and long-term volunteer opportunities (no fee for long term) are available in the SKIP library providing library drop-in services, homework help, and literacy and math programming.

$ Volunteer Partnerships for West Africa

www.vpwa.org

> Volunteer Partnerships for West Africa runs a Street Library Program where volunteers drive a van to a village, set up a tent library, and work with children to develop their literacy skills.

Organizations

American Library Association (ALA): *www.ala.org*

Canadian University Service Overseas (CUSO) E-Volunteering: *www.cusointernational.org/volunteer/types-of-volunteers/e-volunteering*

Council for the International Exchange of Scholars: *www.cies.org/about-us/about-cies*

International Federation of Library Associations and Institutions (IFLA): *www.ifla.org*

Librarians Without Borders (LWB): *http://lwb-online.org*

Libraries Without Borders/Bibliotheques Sans Frontieres: *www.librarieswithoutborders.org*

Mortenson Center for International Library Programs: *www.library.illinois.edu/mortenson*

Peace Corps: *https://www.peacecorps.gov*

United Nations (UN) Volunteers: *https://www.unv.org/*

International Travel Information

Government of Canada: *http://travel.gc.ca/travelling/advisories*

U.S Passports and International Travel:
https://travel.state.gov/content/passports/en/alertswarnings.html

World Health Organization (WHO): *www.who.int/en/*

Note

1. American Library Association, International Relations Office, "International Librarianship Discussion Groups/Listservs," 2017, www.ala.org/aboutala/offices/iro/iroactivities/discussionlists.

bibliography

American Library Association. Discussion lists. www.ala.org/aboutala/offices/iro/iroactivities/discussionlists.

Bordonaro, Karen. *International Librarianship at Home and Abroad.* Cambridge, MA: Chandos, 2017.

Canadian Association of Public Libraries. "Library Advocacy Now! A Training Program for Public Library Staff and Trustees." 2011. cla.ca/wp-content/uploads/LibraryAdvocacyNow.pdf.

Danton, J. Periam. *The Dimensions of Comparative Librarianship.* Chicago: American Library Association, 1973.

Freire, Paulo. *Pedagogy of the Oppressed.* (1970). Translated by Myra Bergman Ramos. New York: Continuum International, 2000.

Go for Hope. "Community Library Projects." 2014. www.goforhope.org/2014/07/23/community-library-projects.

Government of Canada. Travel website. https://travel.gc.ca/travelling/health-safety/diseases/diarrhea.

Grant, Adam. *Give and Take.* New York: Viking, 2013.

———. "The Secret to Success Is Giving, Not Taking." 2013. *Scientific American.* https://www.scientificamerican.com/article/the-secret-to-success-is-giving-not-taking/.

Huffington, Arianna. "Burnout: Time to Abandon a Very Costly Delusion." 2014. www.huffingtonpost.com/arianna-huffington/burnout_b_5102468.html.

Instituto Nacional de Estadística Guatemala, Gobierno de Guatemala. "Caracterización República de Guatemala." 2014. https://www.ine.gob.gt/sistema/uploads/2014/02/26/L5pNHMXzxy5FFWmk9NHCrK9x7E5Qqvvy.pdf.

Irwin, Rachel. "Culture Shock: Negotiating Feelings in the Field." *Anthropology Matters* 9 (2007). https://www.anthropologymatters.com/index.php/anth_matters/article/view/64/123.

Kendall, Sandra. "The Toronto–Addis Ababa Academic Collaboration Library Science Program: A Case Study in Global Librarianship in Ethiopia." In *International Librarianship: Developing Professional, Intercultural, and Educational Leadership*, edited by Constantia Constantinou, Michael J. Miller, and Kenneth Schlesinger, 3–14. New York: State University of New York Press, 2016.

Lakhani, Nina. "Poverty in Nicaragua Drives Children Out of School and into the Workplace." 2015. The Guardian. https://www.theguardian.com/global-development/2015/may/19/poverty-nicaragua-children-school-education-child-labour.

Librarians Without Borders. www.lwb-online.org.

Libraries Without Borders. https://www.librarieswithoutborders.org/about-us.

Libros para Pueblos. www.librosparapueblos.org.

Lor, Peter. "Critical Reflections on International Librarianship." *Mousaion* 25 (2008): 1–15.

———. "International and Comparative Librarianship: A Thematic Approach." 2010. https://pjlor.files.wordpress.com/2010/07/book-front-matter.pdf.

M. K. Gandhi Institute for Non-Violence. 2017. www.gandhiinstitute.org/volunteering-internships/.

Merriam-Webster Dictionary. 2017. https://www.merriam-webster.com.

Nielsen. "Consumer Trust in Online, Social, and Mobile Advertising Grows." 2012. www.nielsen.com/ca/en/insights/news/2012/consumer-trust-in-online-social-and- mobile-advertising-grows.html.

Parker, J. Stephen. "International Librarianship—A Reconnaissance." *Journal of Librarianship* 6, no. 4 (1974): 221.

Partners in Education Roatan (PIER). "Sand Castle Library and Bookmobiles." 2017. www.pierroatan.org.

Pew Research Center. "Social Media Fact Sheet." 2017. www.pewinternet.org/fact- sheet/social-media.

Reitz, Joan M. "Online Dictionary for Library and Information Science." 2004. www.abc-clio.com/ODLIS/odlis_d.aspx.

Sellars, Melanie. "Strategies for Engaging in International Librarianship: Misconceptions and Opportunities." 2016. http://scholarworks.sjsu.edu/slissrj/vol6/iss1/2.

Sharma, Ravindra, ed. *Libraries in the Early 21st Century: An International Perspective*. Boston: De Gruyter Saur, 2012.

Smith, Emily Esfahani. *The Power of Meaning: Crafting a Life That Matters*. New York: Crown, 2017.

Sneed, Rodlescia S., and Sheldon Cohen. "A Prospective Study of Volunteerism and Hypertension Risk in Older Adults." *Psychology and Aging* 28, no. 2 (2013): 578–86.

Storti, Craig. *The Art of Coming Home*. Maine: Intercultural, 2011.

United Health Group. "Doing Good Is Good for You." 2013. www.unitedhealth group.com/~/media/UHG/PDF/2013/UNH-Health-Volunteering-Study .ashx.

U.S. State Department. "Reverse Culture Shock: The Challenges of Returning Home." 2017. https://www.state.gov/m/fsi/tc/c56075.html.

index